At Home in Texas

At Home in Texas

EARLY VIEWS OF THE LAND

By Robin W. Doughty

Texas A&M University Press

COLLEGE STATION

Library of Congress Cataloging-in-Publication Data

Doughty, Robin W.
  At home in Texas.

  Bibliography: p.
  Includes index.
  1. Texas—Description and travel. 2. Land
settlement—Texas—History—19th century. 3. Man—
Influence of environment—Texas—History—19th century.
4. Anthropo-geography—Texas. 5. Texas—Emigration
and immigration. I. Title.
F391.D69 1987   976.4   86-23021
ISBN 0-89096-274-X

Contents

Maps

Acknowledgments

Colleagues both within geography and along its extensive border with liberal arts and the humanities have made suggestions and helpful comments about this research. I thank especially Denis Cosgrove, Jeanne Kay, Terry Jordan, and Robert Mugerauer for offering criticism on the entire manuscript. Tom Cutrer showed me how my English Texan forefathers looked at the land. Don Graham offered an important introduction to regional literature. Stephen Harrigan provided insight and unfailing encouragement. Paul English helped with valuable logistical support. I am also indebted to L. Tuffly Ellis, Alan Friedman, and Dan Luten for advice in discussions about this project, and I appreciate thoughtfulness from departmental colleagues Bharat Bhatt and Ian Manners.

Texas friends have indulged me in my desire to become familiar with the sense of being Texan. They include students Jan Arnold, Douglas Barnett, Karen Hoffman, and Robert Wooster. Another Texan-by-choice, Barbara Parmenter, has made suggestions that served to clarify my thoughts and certainly improved the manuscript. I am most grateful for her assistance.

I thank the staff of the Department of Geography (University of Texas at Austin), Beverly Benadom, Robert Wolfkill, Robert Edwards, and Cathy Hudgins, for the many courtesies in preparing this book. The staff of the Barker Texas History Center, especially Ralph Elder, were interested and most supportive, as were members of the Humanities Research Center. Some of the material has appeared in the *Texas Humanist*.

The University Research Institute under the creative guidance of Dr. William Livingston offered valuable research leave to formulate this study and has supported my efforts along the way. Finally, I am grateful to Linda, Bridget, and Nicho for their understanding and support.

At Home in Texas

1. Introduction

All of us conjure up images of lands that we have heard about, intend to visit, or would like to live in, and retain impressions of those places that we have seen. This book examines the images that native-born American and European settlers formed about Texas and communicated to others from the time of *empresario* land grants after 1820 until roughly the time of the Civil War. Historical information about what people did in taking up new lands in Texas is fairly complete. For instance, we know where farmers and planters moved and what types of crops and animals they brought with them to turn Texas into an agricultural emporium. We also know a good deal about their social life, and especially about the political events that resulted in the Declaration of Independence and eventual annexation by the United States in 1845.

What we need to understand more fully is the set of images that ordinary people carried with them. Texas was an open land, offering free, abundant space for newcomers to occupy and to initiate the routines of clearance, planting, and harvest, routines that they had practiced in other places, even as far away as Western Europe. Most immigrants believed that Texas was a good land—fertile, well watered, abounding in game, and blessed with a climate and soils well suited for agriculture. Everyone recognized that it was a big region—just where its western and northern boundaries lay depended on the political circumstances and claims from the 1830s through the 1850s. Its large areal extent harbored physical diversity; and the best of all places, as we shall see, centered on the area that *empresario* Stephen F. Austin (1793–1836) selected for his first colony. His choice was a natural "parkland," a patchwork of woodlands, openings, and prairies by the alluvium-filled valleys of the Brazos and Colorado rivers. Bigness also appealed to adventurous and curious souls and to ambitious folk who were prepared to move westward into this thinly settled region to secure a bright future for themselves and for their children.

The size and location of Texas, as part of the Hispanic homeland in the Southwest, on the periphery of the American South made distance and physical isolation both a blessing and a curse. Some settlers considered it a blessing, as living there meant freedom from restraints and the opportunity to make something for themselves. Others cursed being so far from relatives and loved ones—and so close to the culturally different Indians and Mexicans.

Human occupation of an area involves providing the basic necessities that keep body and soul together—food, clothes, and shelter. Once these are secured, other concerns surface, including the need to become familiar and comfortable in a new environment and to relate to others in a group or community setting. In this way, newcomers express and satisfy personal goals by articulating and sharing their ideals. Settlement is, therefore, the process of dwelling, of experiencing a sense of belonging in a physical and cultural setting. Human industry transforms a location, a given space, into a place, a repository of meaning. And in establishing this new home, people often refer back to images of other places they have left behind and practice many of the same routines that defined and sustained previous attachments. In entering a new environment and in coming to terms with its features, settlers transpose images of the land with which they are familiar and construct new ones by employing terms that they and others understand. They are anxious to inform relatives and friends about what is the same and about what is different. They employ images that express and satisfy their desire for continuity and also their commitment to this new place.[1]

This book discusses primarily Anglo-American and European images of Texas to bring to light the sense of meaningful connection and participation that they desired in the world. The routines or habits by which this attachment was achieved may have changed, but the aspirations

1. For a discussion of dwelling, see Martin Heidegger, *Poetry, Language, Thought,* pp. 145–61. For its relevance to human geography, see David Seamon, *A Geography of the Lifeworld: Movement, Rest and Encounter;* and Edward Relph, *Rational Landscapes and Humanistic Geography.*

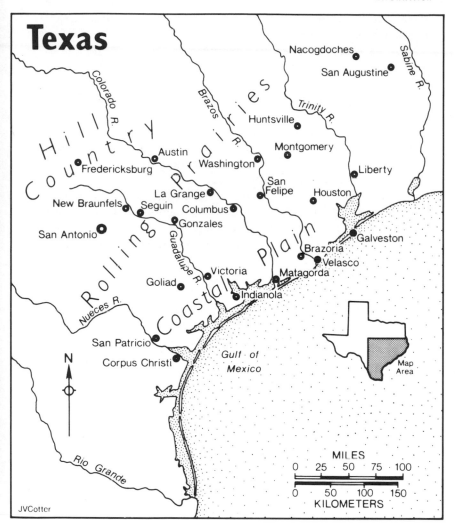

Settlement areas in Texas, mid-nineteenth century.

remain the same: to have a physical and cultural setting in which we may realize our potential as human beings.

More specifically, this book examines commonly expressed ideas, opinions, and beliefs about the land. It deals with how Texas became a special place in the eyes of its settlers, chroniclers, and promoters. Recollections of individual settlers provide explanations about why they came, what they found, and how they intended to turn conditions to their own advantage: in sum, how Texas became their home. Such memories and the images they convey are fundamentally agrarian, and understandably so, as it was mainly farmers, planters, and stockmen who pioneered this frontier zone. The images are also individualistic, fashioned from a belief in personal initiative and enterprise. They are materialistic, emphasizing appropriation and ownership of the land, and exploitation of its natural resources. They are also progressive. These new Texans intended to create a unique society, internally prosperous, free, and democratic.

Native American and Hispanic views of the environment are beyond the scope of this book. This is not because they are unimportant; in fact, American Indian "sacred geography" treats the earth and its resources as having intrinsic rather than instrumental value. New calls are being made to adopt similarly sensitive, ecologically sound ways of looking at and treating the environment. My focus has been directed at those first-, second-, and third-generation, more numerically abundant, Anglo settlers who came to Texas after 1820. Accordingly, prior Spanish and Mexican images have been alluded to from the viewpoint of later, culturally different entrants.[2]

Discussion of land images follows a more thematic than strict chronological sequence, and the images are not peculiar to Texas. Rather, they represent the optimism and energy of people on the nineteenth-century American frontier—more specifically, those individuals who chose to move into the area west of the Mississippi River. Their views of Texas, combining fact with fiction, are shared in some measure by other areas with similar physical and locational characteristics. But they are fundamentally Texan in the sense that they reflect the unique combination of human and physical attributes that has given a distinct personality and heritage to this place in the American Southwest.

Questions of place have long concerned those geographers who re-

2. See J. Donald Hughes, *American Indian Ecology;* and Arnoldo De Leon, *They Called Them Greasers: Anglo Attitudes toward Mexicans in Texas, 1821–1900.*

gard the earth as the home of man. Over the last half century in particular, North American cultural and behavioral geographers have paid increasing attention to the importance of sense of place and of place making. An early exponent, John K. Wright, spoke powerfully about the importance of imagination and perception in understanding human attachment to land, and others have elaborated on the significance of attitudes and perceptions in the dialogue between people and their environment. In a similarly insightful fashion, J. B. Jackson has illuminated the influence of cultural attitudes and values in the shaping of the American landscape.[3]

More recently, several authors have called upon geographers to incorporate a broader concern for individual values and subjective preferences into human geography. In espousing this humanistic approach, they reject the notion of logical positivism (with its methodological insistence on independently verifiable data) as the only acceptable paradigm in the social sciences. Instead they suggest complementing the traditional positivistic method with an experiential approach that would attempt to understand the essence of the human/environment interaction (as lifeworld) through an analysis of the meanings and values with which that interaction is imbued.[4]

Two researchers in particular have attempted to describe and understand the significance to sense of place of the degree and the mode of experiential involvement in lifeworld. Edward Relph has argued in *Place and Placelessness* that participation in the shaping of one's world, either actively or through consensual participation, facilitates the development of an "authentic" sense of place. When the opportunity for such involvement is thwarted, alienation and placelessness result. David Seamon, in a complementary vein, suggests that such authentic involvement is necessary because much of human learning about place is a function of the individual's getting to know places through repeated interactions with them.[5]

Although the number and variety of publications advocating and explaining the experiential approach to sense of place demonstrate the appeal of such research, that approach has been the subject of many

3. John K. Wright, "Terrae Incognitae: The Place of Imagination in Geography," *Annals of the Association of American Geographers* 37 (1947): 1–15; and John B. Jackson, *American Space: The Centennial Years, 1865–1876.*

4. Anne Buttimer, "Grasping the Dynamism of the Lifeworld," *Annals of the Association of American Geographers* 66 (1976): 277–92.

5. Edward Relph, *Place and Placelessness;* Seamon, *Geography of the Lifeworld.*

criticisms. One of the most frequently voiced concerns the lack of empirical data. To be useful, a methodology or research philosophy must be capable of application, and it is to that concern that the present book is addressed. By focusing on American and European settlement of Texas, this study attempts to reconstruct and understand the development of attachment to place by a particular group of people in a specific time and space.

This study contributes to humanistic geography by seeking to convey people's images of Texas and their attraction to it and their commitment to making it that special place, home. It portrays personal geographies, that is, the lives and subjective concerns about the land of some of the individuals who ventured into an unfamiliar setting. It also appreciates the circumstances and conditions that groups of settlers confronted there. Residents altered or modified their initial impressions as they grew familiar with this new land and as they faced, coped with, and survived specific problems in making a home.

Stephen F. Austin's description of Texas as a little-known "wilderness" inhabited by hostile Indians, for example, challenged pioneers to subdue the land and bring it under the control of civilized society. Some settlers were attracted by this idea of besting the wilderness adversary, just as their ancestors had done along the Atlantic seaboard. On the other hand, many men and women were eager to live in wild Texas. Wilderness was itself attractive. Settlers, mostly from Tennessee, the Carolinas, and Arkansas, knew how to make ends meet on a day-to-day basis in this natural place. They survived cold, damp, drought, and flood because they had lived off the land before. The new opportunity of inhabiting Texas, therefore, involved the practice of skills that they had acquired growing up in other regions. They became committed to the Texas wilderness as their new home.

Pioneer Texas families, the so-called Old Three Hundred, proved a tough and hardy lot. They did not back off from a fight with predators, including humans, and survived diseases, storms, and temperature extremes that sapped body and spirit, In this sense, these first agriculturalists were companions of the Mountain Men—symbolic figures in the Wild West—and they popularized the American interior. People heard about such independent-minded Texans and spun tales about their exploits; the Alamo enshrined the myth of doughty warriors. But they were ordinary men and women, each with a tale to tell.

Others in their turn gathered practical information from pioneers. They learned where good lands lay, where to hunt particular animals, and how to avoid or deal with Indians. Often they stayed in the rough cabins thrown up by the first settlers in the Austin Colony until, having gleaned as much information as possible about the lay of the country, and having struck up neighborly bonds, they signed contracts for land and set out on their own.

These southern folk, some with slaves, girdled, cut, and burned trees; split rails; constructed cabins; raised stock; and planted crops. Some were more energetic, successful, or fortunate than others in pushing back the wilderness, and their children inherited a refashioned landscape that reflected the growing imprint of human endeavor.

Where Europeans have gone, they have tended to fashion native vegetation, soils, and fauna into landscapes that resemble their homelands, importing useful plants and animals and adopting indigenous domesticates. It was no different in Texas. Southerners, whose fathers and grandfathers had crossed the Atlantic Ocean, felled and burned immense tracts of cane-filled bottomlands to grow sugar and cotton. Tractable woodland soils soon supported corn, beans, squash, and sweet potatoes in place of native trees and shrubs. Domesticated hogs, many of which soon went wild, rooted for acorns, berries, and nuts, suppressing the regeneration of indigenous plants. Later, on the prairies in the west and north, bison, pronghorn antelope, mustangs, predatory wolves, and even prairie dogs proved obstacles to stockmen who "redeemed the country from the Indians [and] thinned out wild beasts" to claim grasslands for their cattle and sheep.[6]

This customary cycle of clearing the land, planting, tending, and harvesting went hand in hand with Stephen F. Austin's image of a Texas redeemed from primeval chaos and waste. After about 1830, as the wilderness receded, another image grew attractive and popular as authors began to describe Texas in more aesthetic and seductive terms. Physically, more and more of it resembled a garden, they explained, where the seeds of civic virtues and rural arts would surely blossom through the march of civilization. This humanly produced landscape, reclaimed from aboriginal chaos, was stocked with useful plants and animals; settlements embraced by warm, semitropical fertility flourished. Some commentators went so far as to argue that, from the beginning, all or most of Texas was a veritable garden of natural resources—the aboriginal "parkland." The natural richness of soils, abundant water,

6. J. Evetts Haley, *The XIT Ranch of Texas and the Early Days of the Llano Estacado,* pp. 205–206; quotation from *Tascosa Pioneer,* March 30, 1887.

a wealth of native plants and animals made exploitation and "improvements" relatively simple and easy. One's duty, therefore, was to effectively tap and harness such God-given resources. Whether this image of a garden, recently called the feminine emblem of fecundity in the American experience, was conjured up by simple embellishments to a pre-existing "Eden," or whether it was a domesticated landscape hewn from wilderness, this Texas reflected similarities with prior classical landscapes in southern Europe and the Mediterranean.[7]

The image of Texas as North America's own Mediterranean region lent a special romantic quality to the garden myth. On the furthest reaches of the English-speaking world in the United States there existed a region in which settlers planted a wonderful mixture of mid-latitude and subtropical crops. Here was a unique place where Anglo-Saxon enterprise, grafted onto an earlier Spanish agrarian and civic tradition, created a new order. Texas, southern yet western, Anglo-American yet Mexican, was to be America's equivalent of Europe's Mediterranean, and superior to it. Who could fail to commit themselves to making Texas their home?

Were these images of Texas as a Mediterranean, or as a fertile garden and pastoral retreat, or as a primeval wilderness to be conquered, an effective device in attracting settlers and sustaining their efforts? Did settlers, travelers, or prospective residents take any or all of these images seriously, and did they act on them? The answers to these questions about the pull of Texas as it was and as it promised to be, and the experience of Texas as a new home, depend in large part on examination of the recollections of settlers and visitors from about 1820 on. What they said is available from a large number of books, guides, articles, journals, and newspaper columns. There are, of course, promoters to be kept in mind. Authors of *Emigrant Guides* invariably had an interest in selling lands in Texas, and the more land they sold, the more money they made. The same holds true, to a lesser extent, for visitors who penned books about their travels. Irish-born William Kennedy, for example, wrote a widely read text in the 1840s that boosted Texas and Texans, but he had a financial interest in bringing settlers to the region. Other visitors hoped to recoup expenses by writing about distant places and took care to make their experiences remarkable and vivid. Correspondents are most useful because in writing to friends and family, their

---

7. Annette Kolodny, *The Lay of the Land;* and idem, *The Land before Her: Fantasy and Experience of the American Frontier, 1630–1860.*

opinions and suggestions have a spontaneity and sincerity in narrating firsthand experiences. Their high expectations tended to be sobered, or even dashed, by the day-to-day grind of finding and traveling along routes in unfamiliar country. Some diaries and letters from "on the road" reflect the dourness of the immediate situation: disorientation, cold weather, hunger, fatigue, and dyspepsia—circumstances that usually proved transitory and that improved as the journey progressed. Comments, concerns, and wishes in such letters and diaries are important personal appraisals of life in early Texas. They are a rich literature from which to construct "personal geographies" and the experiences of dealing with the changing conditions of land and life.

What did poorly educated folk, unable to read and write, who trudged into East Texas from Arkansas or Louisiana in search of a new start, say and think? How important was the idea of a romantic garden or of Texas as "Italy" to these settlers? Were such images appealing only to foreigners or well-heeled travelers? There are two ways of tackling these concerns of the common man. First, the distinction between an elite, literary viewpoint and a popular, rustic one should not be forced. Ordinary people may not have been able to read or write well, but certainly they conversed with others who could read and did. In discussions about the decision to move to Texas and in setting out, pioneers and their families talked about the situation at staging points along various trails and in settlements. As Texas became better known, popular journals and newspapers carried useful information to American readers stricken by "Texas fever," and even to foreigners infected with the urge to immigrate to America.

Therefore, any hard and fast separation between literary opinion and popular belief cannot be made. In practice, immigrants referred to literature about Texas in conversations with friends and kinfolk who frequently remembered "a book" or carried a yellowed clipping about the prospects and advantages of settlement. The *Arkansas Gazette,* for example, carried with increasing frequency after 1825 information about conditions in the Austin Colony and about methods of obtaining land.

In discussing agriculturalists, a geographer has proposed that "verbal art," often given the pejorative label "folklore," should be included in studies of the consciousness of common folk toward home and habitat. He eschews the condescension of outsiders who label peasants as inevitably dull-witted, stolidly pragmatic, inarticulate, or oblivious of design and beauty. This position is important. It is necessary to feel empathy and gain insight for the lifeworld of ordinary men and women.

Accordingly, I have excluded no source material; rather, I have perused a range of material, including diaries, letters, pamphlets, biographies, and such, written by people of diverse backgrounds.[8]

Some Texans who left accounts of their lives undoubtedly sought a haven from creditors or from the law, but their decision to move involved images and impressions, however wide of the mark, of what Texas was like and what it promised to be. Most settlers looked for cheap and abundant land; they looked for good soils, a healthy climate, personal freedom, or a combination of these things. Such hopes coalesced into a broader picture of a landscape that people journey to, transform, and reorganize. They fulfilled their individual dreams by putting down roots to provide a better life for themselves and their children.

Ultimately, many of these people made a home in Texas and attached themselves to this new land. Various accounts show us how different routines of work and rest helped them define their roles, offering a sense of well-being and harmony with the land. Homes and cabins served as specific foci for this process of attachment. Families adjusted to the layout of their land claims; they grew familiar with the peculiarities of the environment—topography, soils, aspect, plants, and animals—and came to know neighbors and people in distant communities. As human numbers multiplied, and as first-generation Texans matured, breaking away in their turn to build a future, the lived-in quality of the countryside presented a more secure prospect, both visibly in the expansion of the man-altered or cultural landscape, and figuratively in prospects for social progress and personal success.

This feeling of "belonging to Texas," or of becoming "Texan," grew out of a well-practiced agrarian life cycle, which can be glimpsed from autobiographies and recollections. "They were in no hurry to make money and get rich," declared an old-timer from Leon County, situated above the Camino Real between the Trinity and Brazos rivers. He believed that "they enjoyed more real pleasures, were better contented, and were in close[r] contact with life on natural lines" than in 1901, when he penned his recollections. We must recognize that life was not one of "Arcadian simplicity," dreamed up in this old man's mellow years, but we also must understand that many settlers regarded land in the time-honored way as something to be worked with, something that claimed as much from you as you did from it in the course of clearing, stocking, and tilling.

8. Edmunds V. Bunkše, "Commoner Attitudes toward Landscape and Nature," *Annals of the Association of American Geographers* 68 (1978): 551–66.

Also, land was to be tended and accommodated; it drew on reserves of energy and strength, and it often demanded a sacrifice from which only a later generation would benefit.[9]

Novelists capture most effectively this image of rural Texas as a special place, a home that was won and enjoyed by dint of hard, honest work and place-making routines. They, and their literary predecessors who have left yellowed journals or fragmentary accounts of those first years, or who talked to first- and second-generation Texans about old times, provide insights into what the practice of occupation and settlement comprised, and what satisfied the spirit—that yearning in every individual to create something and to leave a mark. We tend to think of these early folk as epic figures as we recall heroic names, places, and events and instill them in our children's minds. But most of these men and women were ordinary people, concerned about making a living and providing for the future. This book records their ideas about the land they settled and the hopes they articulated in making the place called Texas an abiding home.

9. W. D. Wood, "Sketches of the Early Settlement of Leon County," *Southwestern Historical Quarterly* 4 (1901): 214.

2. *Empresario* Texas:
Austin's Redemption of a Wild Land

When Stephen F. Austin complied with his father's dying request that he take up the Spanish land grant, Texas was a relatively empty land. The remote province of newly independent Mexico had only a few thousand Mexican and Indian residents clustered around the presidio of San Antonio de Béxar and its missions, around Bahía or Goliad, in the village of Nacogdoches close to the Sabine River border with Louisiana, and along the Lower Rio Grande Valley and in El Paso.

Early in the nineteenth century Texas was just another sprawling Spanish frontier province, "part mission, part fort, remote, and half forgotten."[1] An 1804 census reported 4,051 people, seven missions, and two presidios. Agriculturalists grew a little corn and smaller quantities of cotton and sugarcane. Livestock totaled eighty-three hundred steers, sixty-five hundred sheep, four thousand horses, and smaller numbers of goats, hogs, and mules. A "lack of skilled men and capital" precluded mineral extraction, so that the Spanish government had been slow in developing the agricultural and mineral properties of this potentially rich region in spite of almost a century of occupation. Citizens in San Antonio planted corn, beans, chili peppers, and some sugarcane; they hunted migratory buffalo in May and October and captured wild horses. It was very much a subsistence economy.[2]

---

1. C. Norman Guice, "Texas in 1804," *Southwestern Historical Quarterly* 59 (1955): 46.
2. Ibid., p. 55; and Mattie A. Hatcher, *The Opening of Texas to Foreign Settlement, 1801–1821*, pp. 303–305.

Not much had changed when Austin arrived in that city almost twenty years later to survey possible sites for colonization. However, after about a decade, Austin's colony on the lower watersheds of the Colorado and Brazos rivers east of San Antonio, in the buffer zone between Hispanic and Anglo-French cultures, totaled almost six thousand residents, many of whom worked farms or plantations on the banks of rivers and creeks. Texas presented a challenge and an opportunity for Stephen F. Austin. The challenge lay in redeeming it from a wild condition. This huge and largely unknown place resembled, both physically and symbolically, the "howling wilderness" that Pilgrims and Puritans had encountered in their first settlement of New England. The land's undeveloped character and enormous spatial extent was recognized by *empresario* Austin as an unprecedented opportunity. Where else could one find such fertile land that, through a combination of political circumstances, had been made suddenly available for non-Hispanic settlers? The opportunity to exploit nature's fecundity in order to establish a permanent, well-ordered society in this vast, far-flung region of Mexico's northeast was unique, he argued, but first one had to subjugate the wilderness.

It was this image of a Texas-to-be that guided the whole colonization enterprise of this "Father of Texas," and the effort to transform the natural landscape into a cultural landscape engaged his constant attention. It was, he said, "a wilderness wholly destitute of resources, the Gov^t unsettled, the Mexicans were gen^{ly} very much prejudiced against North am^n emigration." But he knew what he wanted his colony to become; as acolytes of a new order, his colonists, so-called Texians, would fashion the wilderness into farms and plantations. And after the first five years or so, Austin was certain that by quiet perseverance, "this country will present a second Eden to posterity—wheither *we* shall find it such or not depends on the progress of emigration and improvements."[3]

Two themes guide my examination of Austin's enterprise and pioneering skills. First, it is useful to place this settlement initiative in the broader context of the perceived capabilities of humans to locate and transform environments in the early 1800s. In other words, we must survey briefly ideas about the role of people in making long-term changes to the biological and visible character of landscapes. Second, it is impor-

3. Stephen F. Austin to W. H. Wharton, April 24, 1829, in Eugene C. Barker, ed., "The Austin Papers," *Annual Report of the American Historical Association for the Year 1922 in Two Volumes* (hereafter cited as "Austin Papers"), 2:208; and Austin to James F. Perry, March 31, 1828, ibid., p. 29.

tant to discuss how Austin employed the idea of wilderness to affirm the ability of humans to change the face of Texas and to inspire his colonists toward this goal.

Today the idea of "man's role in changing the face of the earth" goes unchallenged, but a century and a half ago it was novel. One common view held that human capabilities were subordinated to a stronger force—that of an environment or living space that produced and directed the types and levels of civilization. In other words, the physical setting of a region, exemplified by its climate, topography, and location with respect to other places, determined the appearance and character of inhabitants and human culture and set limits on man's activities. In this thinking, mankind was a product of the earth.

Environmental determinism pervaded both popular literature and scientific thought. Medical practitioners in Western culture from the time of Hippocrates in the fourth century B.C. thought of disease as an imbalance of bodily humors associated with the four elements of water, air, fire, and earth. Accordingly, they explained the national character of people by reference to the quantities of moisture or heat in specific localities. Human movements could also be explained by environmental constraints. Drought and pestilence spurred people to leave homelands and invade neighboring territories; natural disasters such as earthquakes and floods, which took heavy tolls, were interpreted as signs of a disordered universe or of divine wrath. In short, mankind was conditioned by the environment and was victim of the vicissitudes of weather and disease that nature visited upon it.

British geologist Charles Lyell (1797–1875), who made two visits to the United States and traveled as close to Texas as New Orleans, expressed a strong belief in determinism. In the first American edition of his *Principles of Geology* (1837), this Oxford-educated expert made it clear that "the aggregate force exerted by man is truly insignificant when we consider the operations of the great physical agents, whether aqueous or igneous, of the inanimate world."[4]

It is not surprising, then, that ten years earlier Stephen F. Austin's letters reflected fatalism about being tested by the environment. The fear that a hard, often short, life in contact with the frontier debased people's character, values, and moral fiber is an established theme in

4. A review of environmentalism is found in Clarence J. Glacken, *Traces on the Rhodian Shore;* Charles Lyell, *Principles of Geology: Being an Inquiry How Far the Former Changes of the Earth's Surface Are Referable to Causes Now in Operation,* 2:111.

American literature and letters. Austin frequently referred to this condition of chaos and savagery in judgments about Texas under Spain's colonial domination. The generic idea of wilderness was, therefore, the benchmark against which he measured the advance of his own colony.

The peculiar location of Texas wilderness posed extra difficulties. The province lay beyond the Mississippi River, two or three days by ship from New Orleans. A foreign government held final say as to where settlers could go and how much land each one received. In such a distant, foreign, and unknown land, settlers had to cope with a hostile environment, plus unusual solitude and isolation.

Ten years after Austin's premature death, Sam Houston had many of the same misgivings grounded firmly in the settlement experience and recent political turmoil. Houston, the Republic's first president, recognized that the wilderness demanded a pioneer's "heart's blood." He or she had to shed it to "prepare the country for their posterity."

Houston embraced cultural over environmental determinism and combined it with ethnic self-consciousness. "Nothing can prevent our mighty march," he charged, because the "contagion of land loving proves irrepressible to the Americans." The image of subduing the land by reducing it to a human, manageable scale so that it reflected industry and enterprise fascinated him. He noted, "If you undertake to go into the wilderness, into the domain of the wild beast, and begin to pursue the game, to plant plantations—when you see the farm, the field, the garden, springing up around you, your feelings will become attached to the land; it will imbue your hearts; you will catch the contagion of the frontier settler; you will not be able to escape it."[5]

In the 1820s, Austin was capitalizing on the land-fever contagion and channeling it. He took pains to ensure that the first settlers carried with them character references. The ability to endure hardship and ward off hostile Indians depended on the strength of will, tenacity, and spirit of cooperation among settlers. Expelling "lawless fugitives" and encouraging "farmers of good character or mechanics" was an important step for this Father of Texas in changing the image from man beleaguered and isolated by nature to man sure of his own abilities and destiny, an image Houston later celebrated.

Successful subjugation of the wilderness, as we shall see, was another way of responding to the charge of human degeneracy. Through "noise-

5. Amelia W. Williams and Eugene C. Barker, eds., *The Writings of Sam Houston, 1813–1863*, 5:34.

less perseverence and industry," said Austin, nature would be forced to unlock its bounties so that "the axe, the plough and the hoe would do more than the rifle or the sword." This was his key to human prosperity and the establishment of civilization.[6]

The second theme of this chapter involves the image of "wilderness" in incipient settlement. Austin used the phrase "redeeming the wilderness" frequently; in published correspondence between 1828 and 1832, for example, he claimed to have confronted and beaten the Texas "wilderness" adversary. It is interesting to examine this image of Texas as a wild, hostile land, to speculate about the *empresario's* use of the term "wilderness," and to contrast it with the later image of Texas as a natural garden.

Georges-Louis Leclerc, Count of Buffon (1707–1788), was one of the first prominent scientists to affirm that humans were indeed capable of transforming environments and "improving" them by occupation, as Austin steadfastly believed. This eighteenth-century luminary produced a widely read forty-four-volume *Histoire naturelle,* which portrayed man as a caretaker or steward of creation. His optimistic picture of the role of mankind in changing the appearance of the earth for the better was the most comprehensive statement in Western thought to his day.

Buffon's *Des époques de la nature,* which first appeared in 1778, presented a teleological vision of civilization perfecting and crowning the environment. As master of the environment it was man's duty to transform and thereby improve nature. The final epoch of earth history, namely Buffon's time (and Austin's as well), represented the development and spread of culture that would harness nature and improve conditions for mankind. Colonization and settlement were intrinsically beneficial processes that ameliorated extremes of climate and, at the same time, turned wild, unkempt environments into useful and beautiful pastures and croplands.[7]

This optimistic vision of man effecting significant landscape change contrasts sharply with another assessment of human activities in the American environment, published nearly thirty years after Stephen F.

6. Stephen F. Austin to ———, July 1, 1821, "Austin Papers," Vol. 1, pt. 1, pp. 399, 400; and Austin to Thomas F. Leaming, June 14, 1830, "Austin Papers," 2:413.

7. Clarence J. Glacken, "Count Buffon on Cultural Changes of the Physical Environment," *Annals of the Association of American Geographers* 50 (1960): 1–21, especially pp. 2–3.

Austin's death. U.S. diplomat George Perkins Marsh, in his *Man and Nature* (1864), provided a discussion of human agency, sparked by modern-sounding condemnation about the negative effects of settlement and the tendency of people to destroy and simplify biological systems. Marsh argued that man was a destroyer of plants and animals, and he challenged Lyell's determinism theory. In later editions of his *Principles of Geology,* Lyell revised his opinions by acknowledging that human population growth diminished both the number and diversity of habitats for native flora and fauna.[8]

This contemporary stance, calling for care, forethought, and understanding of human linkages with the environment, has its roots in Marsh and his successors after the Civil War. Two generations earlier, however, Austin, like Buffon before him, deeply believed that man's transformation of the environment could only be for the better.

But Buffon's special reference to North America was profoundly disturbing. He judged that American animals were not only fewer in number, but also smaller in stature than similar organisms in the Old World. Experts had discovered, he claimed, that European livestock appeared to degenerate after being transported to the American colonies. The basic reason for such physiological deterioration was the environment. People were only beginning to introduce European agricultural improvements into North American settlements; as a consequence, wild nature, scarcely touched by human endeavor, remained "weaker, less active, and more circumscribed in the variety of her productions." Life had not prospered "under a niggardly sky and an unprolific land, thinly peopled with wandering savages"; it required sustained, dedicated human enterprise to reclaim it.[9]

Buffon did not look on America as the earthly paradise that some sixteenth-century navigators described; instead, he presented the landscape as a dismal scene requiring the industry of man to dignify it. Buffon's supporters and commentators included humans in their picture of American degeneracy. Some claimed that colonists were "less robust in labour, less powerful in war, and less adapted to the arts than their ancestors."[10]

---

8. George Perkins Marsh, *Man and Nature: Or, Physical Geography as Modified by Human Action;* and Lyell, *Principles of Geology,* 11th ed., rev., 2:457.

9. Gilbert Chinard, "Eighteenth Century Theories on America as a Human Habitat," *Proceedings of the American Philosophical Society* 91 (1947): 31.

10. Ibid., p. 37.

Austin, in the manner of Franklin and Jefferson, countered this pessimistic picture of degeneracy by emphasizing the region's resource variety, biological exuberance, and suitability for human occupation. In his appeals for additional settlers, he continually emphasized that truly fine lands awaited those honest farmers and planters whom he needed to "calmly put their shoulders to the wheel and toil for the good of others as well as for their own." He wished to encourage "that class of emigrants who deserve the appellation of southern Gentlemen" and, as the years passed, he was more confident about the character and quality of those men and women who had chosen Texas as their home.[11]

Referring to America, Franklin and Jefferson praised the nation's fecundity and its abundance of resources in their direct challenge to Buffon. Scholars have noted how government-sponsored expeditions from Lewis and Clark's time onward provided details about the grandeur of the continent's interior—Yellowstone River and the canyons, hot springs, and geysers, Yosemite Valley and the subliminal landscapes of the Rockies—that matched, or bettered, anything in Europe. The Old World was without hummingbirds, bald eagles, ivory-billed woodpeckers, and other unusual animals that ornithologists Alexander Wilson and John James Audubon popularized. Scientists and politicians were able, therefore, to contrast an abundant, colorful, and varied fauna in North America with a more somber one in Europe.[12]

This humanistic vision of America's natural wonders was also a romantic one. It impressed foreign travelers and many early settlers, including Texans. Some believed that Texas was already a garden of many different natural resources. Others recognized that the garden needed to be cleared and tended to banish the mystery, chaos, and danger of the wilderness, which was not the most suitable habitat for satisfying food, shelter, and other needs. Austin shared both viewpoints, but emphasized the latter. Confronting wild nature and struggling to clear and plant the garden of Texas-to-be concerned him most of all in the fifteen years he spent as patriarch of his burgeoning colony between the banks of the Brazos and Colorado rivers. Austin's belief about his mission, the rhetoric he used to popularize it, and his assessment of the amount of progress toward a new order recall the Pilgrim and Puritan call-to-

11. Austin to W. H. Wharton, April 24, 1829, "Austin Papers," 2:208, 212; and Austin to Thomas White, March 31, 1829, ibid., p. 198.

12. Chinard, "Eighteenth Century Theories," pp. 41–42; and William H. Goetzmann, *Exploration and Empire,* pp. 330–31, passim.

arms in incipient colonization efforts in New England some two hundred years earlier. His outlook reflects the medieval outlook of attacking the wilderness that stretches back in Europe to Neolithic times.

As promoter and leader, Austin single-mindedly dedicated himself to instructing others about the trials and tribulations of wilderness living. Problems included threats to life and health that made nature the villain in what some scholars have termed the "morality play" between forces of good and evil in the settlement of the West.[13]

The Texas Wilderness

Austin's recognition of Texas as a future home rested on two separate but interrelated ideas. First, there was the need to carve out a physical space for a new community in a thinly inhabited, uncharted, and strange land. Second, he and other people recognized that the region consisted of fertile soils, abundant water, and useful plants and animals. Abundant natural resources provided the foundation of his colony.

We shall examine the process of environmental transformation or wilderness clearance and Austin's perception of his role as a Boone-like patriarch seeing to the many details and problems of day-to-day activities in such a remote region. His sense of duty never wavered or diminished. In fact, this promotor's concern about his responsibilities to settlers increased as the political circumstances of his fledgling colony grew more difficult and complex. A large portion of the financial burden of administering this new experiment consumed the *empresario*'s energy and resources. Austin undertook lengthy travels, withstood imprisonment in Mexico, and suffered misunderstanding at home, all because he burned with a desire to secure a future for his colony.

Austin's decision to establish a settlement in the "middle zone" of Texas was judicious. His land grant included the watersheds of the Brazos and Colorado rivers between the colonial Hispanic system of San Antonio de Béxar in the west and the woodland settlement of traders, farmers, and adventurers around Nacogdoches in the east. It is clear that he knew his geography and felt a compelling drive to exploit its resources. Austin, his colonists, and later settlers celebrated the basic fecundity of the undulating or rolling prairie zone of interior Texas and

13. Louis B. Wright, *Culture on the Moving Frontier*, p. 11.

pushed into the flat zone next to the coast, where some of the richest plantations existed. "Texas as a Country . . . may be advantageously compared with any portion of North America," he declared enthusiastically. Its soils were "productive beyond expectation"; many rivers were "navigable, and our harbors safe," and the climate was "healthy and pleasant."[14]

Rich soil, superior pastures, beneficent climate, proximity to the sea, and "other natural advantages" were apparent to Austin on his first visit to Texas, when he explored a large tract of south-central Texas oak and pine woodland and the coastal plain. His party of a dozen or so men traveled between the Sabine River and Nacogdoches, an area they likened to the Kentucky Barrens. Once past that stretch of redlands, named after the color of the soil, they crossed the Trinity River and filched one and a half gallons of honey from a bee tree. Thereafter, the country slowly opened up with wider and more frequent prairies, proving agreeable in aspect and plentiful in game.[15]

On his first day in Texas, Austin found the area west of the Sabine River abounding in luxuriant grasses. Landscapes became visually more compelling as he moved onward. A beautiful prairie beyond the Trinity River was "covered with the highest and thickest growth of grass I ever saw." Near the Brazos River he made the pithy comment, "very good, rolling Prairie black soil, sufficiently timbered." Such notes typified Austin's keen eye for promising country; he was looking for especially fertile places. "Grapes in immense quantities" hung from trees on the banks of the Colorado River; the floodplain of the San Marcos River looked suitable for irrigation, and near the Guadalupe River stretched a rolling country, "the most beautiful I ever saw."[16]

Austin learned a great deal from this midsummer foray into south-central Texas and was especially impressed by the basins of the Brazos, lower Guadalupe, and Colorado rivers, in which his party encountered large numbers of deer, wild cattle, and mustangs. Texas teemed with wild animals that symbolized nature's prodigality. Austin hunted them while he assessed soils, vegetation, and water.

14. Stephen F. Austin to J. L. Woodbury, July 6, 1829, "Austin Papers," 2:227.

15. Stephen F. Austin to [Joseph H. Hawkins], July 20, 1821, "Austin Papers," Vol. 1, pt. 1, p. 403; and [Stephen F. Austin], "Journal of Stephen F. Austin on His First Trip to Texas, 1821," *Quarterly of the Texas State Historical Association* 7 (1904): 286–307, especially p. 293.

16. "Journal of Stephen F. Austin," pp. 294–96.

This image of a superabundant, primitive, "good" land lasted a long time. Foreign travelers were awed and inspired by this Texas, as were promoters. Even the acerbic, patronizing British diplomat Francis Sheridan had no doubts about natural resources and fertility, although he had grave reservations about the character of its inhabitants.[17]

But colonists needed food, and though Austin judged his grant to be "so much more valuable than I expected," he referred constantly to the fundamentally wild, untouched, and unknown character of the land. It required clearing and cultivating to become a home. "When I explored this country in 1821, it was a wild, howling, interminable solitude from Sabine to Bexar," Austin admitted. Civilization was confined to a few isolated missions and military outposts. He recognized that Mexican officials knew almost nothing about the province, being "profoundly ignorant of its real value, and also that they considered it next to impracticable to form a settlement in its wilderness" without strong military support.[18]

This wilderness motif, commonly expressed during colonization endeavors on the New England seaboard, occurs frequently in Austin's letters. He was proud of coming face to face with the mysterious, elemental forces of the Texas frontier and doing battle with them. Coming to grips with the wilderness was a challenge unique to Americans. It represented the individual's right and responsibility to succeed. It also symbolized the spiritual battle of a chosen Protestant people whose destiny was to found a new civilization—a promised Canaan—in a vast, unkempt, and strange region. Consequently, the wilderness of frontier America as it was pushed beyond the Appalachians into the Ohio Valley and across the Mississippi River was actually the battleground for forces of order, reason, and culture versus others of chaos, instinct, and beastliness. Land promoters and their settlers on the remote Texas frontier waged a war for the environment's natural bounty, but first they had to win their battles and subjugate their adversary, nature. Austin's frequent reference to conquering the wilderness, therefore, was in the mainstream of the American Protestant colonization endeavor. Texas presented a difficult opponent. In physical terms, it was vast and en-

17. Willis W. Pratt, ed., *Galveston Island; or, a Few Months off the Coast of Texas: The Journal of Francis C. Sheridan, 1839–1840*, p. 37.

18. Stephen F. Austin to Mary Austin Holley, November 17, 1831, "Austin Papers," 2:705; and Austin to Thomas F. Leaming, June 14, 1830, ibid., p. 414.

vironmentally complex. Furthermore, no American had gained official permission to settle there from the foreign government that ruled this wild, unpeopled land.

Austin's upbringing in a household with roots in Puritan New England and his early education in Connecticut most probably played a role in his vision of Texas in terms of wilderness redemption. A number of previous occupations, including businessman, legislator, and judge, proved extremely useful on the Texas frontier, where Mexican authorities invested him with unprecedented powers. This capable, well-educated "patriarchal ruler of a wilderness commonwealth" possessed a well-developed sense of obligation and responsibility for his Texas settlement. Austin's belief in a calling, rules for settlers, judgments about conditions, and hopes for the future recall the admonition of New England's Puritans. They were sure that destiny called them to their peculiar errand into the wilderness, an errand that became so central to the American experience.[19]

Lamentations and calls for repentance from the Boston Synod in 1679 were echoed in Austin's letters and commentaries 150 years later. Originally, denunciations included twelve listings in decay of godliness among second- and third-generation New Englanders. Headings included pride and insubordination, conspicuousness in dress, foul language, lying, contentiousness, the use of alcohol, "mixed dancings," land speculation, debauchery, and a general loss of morals. Austin's letters to his family and friends reveal many of the same fears, but in another sense he was sure of his calling and wanted to realize it in Texas.[20]

At the outset, Austin advised his mother and sister, whom he wished to live beside him in Texas, to transport simple goods such as household articles and plain clothes. "Let our motto therefore be *economy* and *plain* living," he advised, to set a good example. Schooled by adversity and profiting from hardships, he was sure that prospects would improve, but was determined to have everything in the house "plain and pritty [*sic*] much like the rest of my neighbors."[21]

Austin denounced rancor and dissent, especially directed against Mexican authorities. He went to great lengths to reaffirm in frequent cor-

19. Eugene C. Barker, *The Life of Stephen F. Austin;* idem, "Stephen F. Austin," in *Readings in Texas History,* Barker Papers, Box 2B107, "Articles, 1914–1918," p. 147; and Perry Miller, *Errand into the Wilderness.*

20. Miller, *Errand into the Wilderness,* pp. 7–8.

21. Stephen F. Austin to Mother and Sister, May 4, 1824, "Austin Papers," Vol. 1, pt. 1, p. 785.

respondence with Hispanic officials that both he and his colonists were steadfast citizens of Mexico. It was a position that the *empresario* maintained through the 1820s, until he finally abandoned it when the Mexican government prohibited immigration by U.S. residents, rejected statehood for Texas, and, under Santa Anna, chose the path of repression and conflict.

Austin was a man of abiding pragmatism rather than political zealotry. He has been called "the greatest colonial proprietor in North American history," being immensely skilled in dealing with people — welcoming them to Texas and protecting them from foreign officialdom. He avoided conflict and subordinated his personal interests to those of his colonists. This true gentleman among the total of twenty-six *empresarios* in early Texas was a "visionary, capitalist, developer and Father of his People, all in one," but not everyone recognized the quality of the man.

Disappointment about the public's ingratitude and mistrust of his personal motives and activities dogged Austin throughout his sojourn in Texas. Nothing he did, he claimed, was motivated by a desire for personal aggrandizement in terms of money, fame, or power. He also condemned speculation of any kind and set himself apart from those colonists and land agents who engaged in it. He constantly assured people that his only mission was to found a new order in Texas by transforming wild conditions and to secure a future for his society.

Austin accepted, albeit reluctantly, some rum that had been brewed from molasses at Martin Varner's place in 1829. It was, he believed, the first "ardent spirits of any kind that was ever made in this colony." People drank alcohol, he knew, and he was not averse to a glass or two of wine; therefore, ever the pragmatist, he decided that it was better to manufacture such beverages "at home" than to purchase them expensively elsewhere.[22]

Austin may have tolerated alcohol, but he criticized uncouth characters, among whom he included lawyers, and he endeavored to keep them out of Texas by dealing personally with most legal matters. So completely was his life given over to the colony that Mary Austin Holley chided her laconic cousin to laugh away care, recommending that he socialize more. "I do owe a great and heavy weight of responsibility to my settlers, and to my adopted Government," Austin reiterated; "my

22. T. R. Fehrenbach, *Lone Star: A History of Texas and the Texans,* pp. 145–46, discusses Austin's role; and Austin to Israel Waters, July 30, 1829, "Austin Papers," 2:243.

motto is *Fidelity and gratitude to the Mexican government; and to be true to the interests and welfare of my colonists.*" But on one occasion, after a forty-seven-mile ride on colony business, he admitted to Holley that he had summoned energy to dance with his sister at a gathering and had enjoyed himself.[23]

Mary Holley played an important role in bringing out a part of Austin's personal, suppressed, and very guarded self. He knew that people regarded him as taciturn and aloof. He was often lonely. But letters to Holley enabled him to confide his vision and his hopes, including the intention to retire to a pastoral retreat at the mouth of the Brazos River—a hope he never fulfilled.

Holley helped to fill the "melancholy void" made by the death of Austin's mother, who never reached Texas, and that of his brother John, who died shortly after becoming a resident. At one point, in affectionate correspondence with cousin Mary, Austin's wilderness experience suddenly turned out a romantic wonderland. "On our ponies we will scamper over the flowery prairies to the sea beach, and along it with the wide waste of the ocean on one hand, the level green carpet of nature fringed by distant woods, on the other, and friendship and happiness in our hearts." But it was pure escapism. Concern for the political misfortunes of the early 1830s consumed him, and he saw Holley only rarely before he died.[24]

In Austin's situation it was not simply the reality of man against wilderness and the individual isolated from friends and relatives, thrown back on himself; political problems demanded attention, too, namely, strategies that would mollify the tradition-bound government of Mexico. Austin told Holley and others that his aim was to pursue a "silent" course for settlement. "Texas must be settled silently, or not at all," meaning full subordination to the constraints and restrictions imposed by authorities. The diligent employment of the axe, plow, and hoe, not the sword or rifle, was paramount; the "only means of redeeming this country from the wilderness was by peaceful *silent,* noiseless, perseverance [*sic*] and industry."[25] The *empresario* learned Spanish, traveling to Mexico in his first year to secure legal title to his father's

---

23. Stephen F. Austin to Mary Holley, July 19, 1831, "Austin Papers," 2:675, 677; and Austin to Holley, January 4, 1832, ibid., p. 733.

24. Stephen F. Austin to Mary Holley, January 14, 1832, "Austin Papers," 2:736.

25. Stephen F. Austin to Thomas F. Leaming, June 14, 1830, "Austin Papers," 2:414.

venture. He spent twenty-eight months in the early 1830s as a prisoner of the Mexican government, which suspected him of plotting insurrection.

In addition to recognizing thrift, industry, and honesty in many colonists, Austin felt he was destined to fashion a new American community from the Texas lands. This process of Americanization in North America has links to constant harangues about sin and calls for repentance, especially in Puritan New England. Austin fit a more secular image of the patriarch urging followers to construct the City of God in the wilderness. But he was sure of his covenant, just as Winthrop, Hooker, and Mather had been of theirs. God wished him to redeem Texas.

Austin revealed this belief in an unusual letter. Writing to Holley, he recognized that a person's life was a mere "*speck between two eternities.*" He placed confidence "upon the throne of *one, only just and omnipotant* [sic] *God;* — the God of the eternity past — the speck — and the eternity to come — uncreated." Faith was essential: the faith and confidence in "the self existing, consistent, and bountiful Father of Worlds, of time and of Eternity," he claimed. From such a perspective, Austin, the believer, was able to separate himself from the trials or disappointments of the moment (the threat to terminate all future immigration from the United States), the fallibility of men (they were ungrateful for what he had accomplished), and could face the future with equanimity.[26]

Austin's strategy for turning back the wilderness and redeeming Texas deserves scrutiny. There existed, he said, three stages or "regular gradations" for colonization. The first was to overcome the "roughness" of natural conditions, to be compared with a farmer cutting and clearing land "covered with woods, bushes, and brambles." The next step he likened to "ploughing, harrowing and sowing the ground after it is cleared," which meant laying the foundation for lasting advancement. The third, and most important, step was "gathering in the harvest and applying it to the promotion of human happiness." In January, 1832, when he used this metaphor in a letter to cousin Mary, Austin judged that there was still some clearing to do, but he had already sown much seed and was looking for "the genial influences of Cultivated society . . . like the sun shedding light, fragrance and beauty."[27]

---

26. Stephen F. Austin to Mary Holley, January 4, 1832, "Austin Papers," 2:733.
27. Stephen F. Austin to Mary Holley, January 14, 1832, "Austin Papers," 2:737.

Clearing the Land

Clearing was the first, most important act of redemption. It was the work of the missionary who planted the cross in a new land, pitting the symbol of good against evil, just as it had been in medieval Europe, where the evil woods harbored the last of the old pagan gods, where the "deep, dark forest" of the brothers Grimm was the abode of evil creatures. One expected numerous insecurities and physical hardships, but with a deep faith in a personal, transcendent God, it was possible to work the miracle of conquest.

Austin was sure that he was called to this act of redemption; his tact and patience with disease, difficult settlers, stock thefts by Indians, and floods that wiped out crops, proved remarkable. Often his letters revealed disappointment about specific conditions or circumstances, but he never lost the determination to continue with his mission, employing skill and discrimination in his dealings with distant government officials and disgruntled settlers. The dedication to a task that his father, Moses Austin, had set him is remarkable when one remembers that Stephen was initially reluctant to take up the claim.

Missionary fervor made the conquest itself more important than amassing a personal fortune, becoming recognized for political acumen, or being feared because of the absolute powers that he possessed. The explanation stems, in part, from the *empresario*'s discovery that Texas was more valuable than he had initially believed. "A civilized and industrious population" would improve Texas, in the same sense that Buffon pictured agriculture and industry as improvements to the earth itself. Civilization was developing and expanding in the Southwest.[28]

Austin's enthusiasm for Texas grew also from knowing that the civilization was American. His colony functioned as "a home for the unfortunate, a refuge from poverty, an asylum for the sufferers from selfish avarice." Above all, its population was to "harmonize with their neighbors on the *East*, in language, political principles, common origin, sympathy and even interest."[29]

The first step in clearing demanded the right type of people. He expected immigrants to be honest, nominally Roman Catholic, and prepared to take an oath of allegiance to the Mexican constitution.

28. Stephen F. Austin to Mary Holley, November 17, 1831, "Austin Papers," 2:705.

29. Stephen F. Austin to Mary Holley, December 29, 1831, "Austin Papers," 2:727; and idem, August 21, 1835, in Eugene C. Barker, ed., *The Austin Papers, 1834–1837*, vol. 3 (hereafter cited as *Austin Papers*), p. 101.

Austin's initial agreement with colonists also requested that newcomers assist "in building Cabbins and a Stockage, should one be deemed necessary, and to clear fence, and cultivate at least five acres of corn." Each man received 640 acres as head of a household and a lesser amount for his wife, children, and slaves. A special colonization law made it possible to vary the acreage, depending on whether a man's chief occupation was farming or stock raising. The law enabled Austin to designate lands, almost without limit, to individuals whom he deemed especially deserving.[30]

Austin set his colony "an example of economy and plainness." Woodsmen who had built homes in Tennessee, Kentucky, the Arkansas Territory, and elsewhere joined him, and gradually they transformed the face of the land by cutting and burning woods and canebrakes, exterminating cougars and wolves, and trapping beaver. They pushed back the forest edge, drove off predatory mammals and thieving birds from stock and crops, and loved to hunt. Austin encouraged such loyal folk to work together, like a family, in dutifully reclaiming lands from solitude and unkemptness.[31]

Some people commented about the effects of such reclamation. In June, 1824, colonist Randall Jones hoped that the country would settle fast, but foresaw problems. He suggested that a register be set up for livestock brands and marks and added, "An act to prevent the killing of Deer and wild Horses for the Skins alone I think necessary also." He also observed that carelessly set fires were endangering nearby settlements.

As clearing proceeded, the wilderness began to recede. Frontiersman and Indian fighter Thomas Williams arrived from the Arkansas Territory in December, 1821, and lived off wild meat until the corn that he planted near the Colorado River, below present-day La Grange, produced ten bushels per acre. John Rabb and James Gilleland, also from Arkansas, cleared land upriver from Williams, but pilfering by Indians forced them to move east to a more secure place on the Brazos watershed. Aylett C. Buckner, who was "one of the first men who built a Cabbin on this River [Colorado]," and the first to have had a plow "stuck in the field," claimed that he had "never asked the first Cent for a man

30. Agreement with Emigrants, ca. November 22, 1821, "Austin Papers," Vol. 1, pt. 1, p. 432; and Lester G. Bugbee, "The Old Three Hundred," *Quarterly of the Texas State Historical Association* 1 (1897): 108–17.

31. Stephen F. Austin to Mary Holley, January 14, 1832, "Austin Papers," 2:737.

eating under my Roof and have fed as many and I believe more people than any man," including Austin.[32]

Authors have repeatedly suggested that early settlers like Buckner were generous and hospitable. Austin reassured one doubting correspondent that he would not be robbed and declared that houses and even stores had no fastenings except a wooden pin or door latch. Mustangs were the only "robbers," as they ran off unpenned horses.

Conditions in the colony dictated that people share food, information, and know-how. Some took advantage of this custom. For example, in July, 1822, two men rescued Mrs. James H. Long and her family from a "palmetto camp" open to the sun and rain, constructed a cabin for her, and supplied cornmeal, pork, and salt with the understanding that relatives would fetch her. The two settlers provided horses and food and guided her to San Antonio after the destitute lady told them the governor had sent for her. They wrote to Austin eighteen months later complaining that they remained out-of-pocket and asked him to help settle the debt.[33]

Ties of kinship, friendship, and acquaintance served to solidify bonds between folk who were distributed thinly across east-central Texas. Fear also played a part. People dreaded contagious diseases, but especially the presence of Indians in and around their settlements. Recent scholarship has characterized Austin's redemptive act as including American Indians and Mexicans with other elements of the wilderness to be subdued. The *empresario* and early colonists, however, perceived the aboriginal population as a hindrance to the security of settlement. In his 1821 explorations, Austin called the Cocos and Karankawas "universal enemies to man," for whom there was no means of subjugation except by extermination. Mexican authorities gave him permission to wage war on the Waco Indians, and his 1825 "Memorandum on Indian Relations" claimed that they were stealing horses. Much has been written about the Indian question, including personal and highly colored accounts from those pioneers who grew famous for "chastising" Indians.

32. Randall Jones to Austin, June 4, 1824, "Austin Papers," Vol. 1, pt. 1, p. 809; J. H. Kuykendall, "Reminiscenses of Early Texans, II," *Quarterly of the Texas State Historical Association* 6 (1903): 311–30, especially pp. 320–21; and Aylett C. Buckner to Austin, April 20, 1825, "Austin Papers," Vol. 1, pt. 2, p. 1076.

33. Stephen F. Austin to Thomas White, March 31, 1829, "Austin Papers," 2:199; and Deposition Concerning Mrs. Long, February 26, 1824, "Austin Papers, Vol. 1, pt. 1, pp. 747–48.

For the most part, early Texans excluded Indians or Mexicans from their future Texas.[34]

Austin reminded correspondents that Hispanic policies had allowed Texas to remain in such an undeveloped state. Holley accounted for about thirty-eight hundred Mexicans in the region in 1831, most of them in San Antonio. Some worked for settlers as horsemen, others farmed "on a limited scale," and many captured mustangs to sell to incoming settlers. Holley's answers to questions about Texas from London's Royal Geographical Society implied a second-class status for them.[35]

As part of this initial process of clearing, it is useful to understand what settlers required in the way of household goods, utensils, and other necessities in the Texas wilderness. Austin's requests to his mother and sister, and to other relatives or close friends whom he welcomed to his colony, provide details about objects that normally we take for granted.

Furniture was too heavy to transport long distances; Austin recommended that his family sell most of theirs to purchase enough victuals — pork, flour, beans, and so on — for the entire journey. Beds and bedding, however, were to be carried; also books, for which Austin had a need: "We shall want them to pass away the time." Austin asked for good writing paper and other lightweight objects such as pots, crockery, flannel cloth, ribbons, salts, and "a good Mosquetoe bar." Cottons and linens sold well in Texas, and sugar, tea, coffee, spices, and rice could be obtained en route in Alexandria or Natchez. Barrels of excellent beans or peas were to come from Missouri, the Austin family's point of departure; also hominy, dried apples and peaches, which, if not consumed, would fetch a good price in Natchitoches, a stopping place in Louisiana. On a personal note, Austin asked for "some household cloth for me for summer and winter clothing."[36]

Immigrants bartered food and materials on their journeys, but needed to keep their tools — "a good sett of blacksmith tools," for instance — for use at their destination. Spades, shovels, hand irons, and steel implements proved invaluable. An early colonist, Jesse Burnam, recorded how one farmer, possessing no other implements, had planted his first

34. Arnoldo De Leon, *They Called Them Greasers: Anglo Attitudes toward Mexicans in Texas, 1821–1900*, pp. 1–13.

35. "Journal of Stephen F. Austin," p. 305; and Mary Austin Holley, *Texas*, p. 138.

36. Stephen F. Austin to J. E. B. Austin, May 4, 1824, "Austin Papers," Vol. 1, pt. 1, p. 788; and Austin to Mother and Sister, May 4, 1824, "Austin Papers," Vol. 1, pt. 1, pp. 786–87.

corn crop with a stick. Burnam exchanged a horse and journeyed sixty miles to obtain twenty bushels of corn. With regard to animals and other plants, Austin recommended "a pair or two of Geese and tame ducks," and he wanted "all kind of Gardin Seeds particularly Cabbage, Lettice, beats, Sage-Summer Savery, horse reddish etc, etc." Colonists could pick up orange, fig, and grape roots in Louisiana. He suggested they carry in pear, apple, crab apple seeds, and nectarine and peach stones.[37]

Promoter Austin possessed a lively, abiding interest in horticulture. In a missive to his mother and sister in 1824, he stressed that they bring roots, including those for currants, gooseberries, and roses. In the same decade, he admonished his brother-in-law, James F. Perry, to move to Texas and asked him to "bring all manner, and great quantities of fruit seeds" and gooseberry and raspberry roots. In the late 1820s, conditions had improved; transformation of the wilderness was still proceeding, but life was more comfortable; "fine clothes have taken the place of buckskin."[38]

Plowing and Sowing

Texans prized grape slips, plum stones, and all manner of garden seeds in the 1820s and early 1830s. In one letter, Austin judged that nature seemed to have intended Texas to be a vineyard; native grapes festooned trees along the banks of rivers and creeks. He also included a vineyard in a house plan that he drew up in 1831. The garden and orchard for Austin's imaginary retreat on Chocolate Bayou, a plan of which he sent to his sister Emily, lay east or west of the house along the woodland edge and away from cowpens and stables — doubtless to keep loose stock from consuming the produce. The eleven-room building, which measured about ninety by forty-six feet, included a bee house in the fenced-off horticultural plot. This area was protected from north winds by a line of trees. The hundred-foot front yard between the garden and corral faced south and contained a row of orange

---

37. Jesse Burnam, "Reminiscences of Capt. Jesse Burnam," *Quarterly of the Texas State Historical Association* 5 (1901): 12–18; Austin to Mother and Sister, May 4, 1824, "Austin Papers," Vol. 1, pt. 1, p. 786; and Austin to J. E. B. Austin, May 4, 1824, "Austin Papers," Vol. 1, pt. 1, pp. 788–89.

38. Stephen F. Austin to James F. Perry, December 31, 1829, "Austin Papers," 2:308; and January 3, 1830, p. 318.

trees through which the visitor proceeded to the main veranda of the residence.[39]

Planning the aspect and form of a residence and planting gardens comes into the stage of plowing and sowing. Austin's imaginary estate was to be the base from which he could attend to his settlers' daily needs. In reality, a simple log cabin served this function. Historian Eugene C. Barker, Austin's biographer, spoke eloquently of the enormous task of directing surveys, which Austin often made himself, of writing out grants and keeping records and titles, of dealing with visitors, answering inquiries, and receiving settlers. Austin's many social skills and extraordinary authority as judge, governor, and militia leader in an area about the size of Massachusetts taxed reserves of energy, patience, and tact. But these duties constituted the "planting" of his colony. Austin held legislative, executive, and judicial powers, and after scrutinizing his performance, Barker judged him grave but kindly, tolerant, charitable, and loyal, restrained in habit, often lonely, and probably given to much introspection.[40]

But Austin was both a visionary and a pragmatist. Restraining his impulses, he made careful and considered decisions, one of the most thoughtful being to pursue a "silent" course of settlement in Texas. Firsthand knowledge of Mexican manners and character and of a government that harbored deep mistrust of foreigners, including himself, convinced Austin that any enterprise aimed at permanent agriculture should be understated and inconspicuous, even to neighbors in Louisiana. After a decade, however, he judged that more than a toehold had been gained as several thousand newcomers inhabited the Brazos and Colorado watersheds. The *empresario* decided to "bring out my *ward* and introduce her to the world."[41] With the seed planted, his thoughts turned to the harvest.

Austin's diplomatic capabilities appear in the exemption that he obtained to the law against further U.S. immigration in 1830, and the eventual reversal of that rule in 1833. The number of new Texans entering his colony created a broader settlement base. Industry was moving in. In 1829, Austin wrote enthusiastically to Henry Austin that a steam mill

---

39. Stephen F. Austin to S. Rhoads Fisher, June 17, 1830, "Austin Papers," 2:425; and Austin's House Plans, November 30, 1831, "Austin Papers," 2:715–21.

40. Barker, "Stephen F. Austin," pp. 149, 157.

41. Stephen F. Austin to Mary Holley, November 17, 1831, "Austin Papers," 2:705.

was being constructed on a tidal stream by Galveston Bay. He hoped to open a road to El Paso and Santa Fe and thereby switch trade from Missouri to Galveston, from which connections could be fashioned to Mexico's Sonora and Chihuahua.[42]

Settlers continued to turn back the wilderness. They set out large farms and made "valuable improvements" to an area in which only a few years earlier there had been "not one civilized being within two hundred miles," clarioned Austin. High-quality cotton and sugarcane, and other crops similar to those in Mississippi and Louisiana, flourished in Texas. Cattle, horses, mules, sheep, and hogs thrived; conditions for both plants and animals appeared to exceed expectations. Riparian areas were admittedly subject to fever and agues, but less so than other U.S. rivers "below latitude 36," he added.[43]

Austin was so ebullient in praising the initiative and enterprise of his fellow Texans in setting up a system of agriculture that Barker called it a "fervor of religious devotion." His fervor was fed by the growth and success of his small colony after only a decade in existence. With this perspective, and from firsthand travels, Austin was convinced that Texas' lands possessed greater promise than those in the southern United States. "A few more years and the prosperity of Texas will astonish many," Austin predicted. The third stage, or "harvest," was close at hand.[44]

Harvest

"Harvest," the final step in colonization, provided direction to "public opinion, morality and education; — to give tone, character and consistency to society." In this stage, Austin regarded Texas as "Eden," and the image of the garden replaced that of the wilderness. It crowned the efforts of the better type of settlers who were community-conscious Texans. Clearing and planting provided the fruits of country living and rural discourse. "We will then," said Austin, "arrange our cottages — rural — comfortable — and splendid . . . Gardens and rosy bowers, and ever verdant groves, and music, books, and intellectual amusements can all be ours." This pastoral image resembled passages in southern agri-

---

42. Stephen F. Austin to Henry Austin, August 27, 1829, "Austin Papers," 2:253.

43. Stephen F. Austin to Emily M. Perry, July 24, 1828 "Austin Papers," 2:77; and Austin to David Porter, February 16, 1829 "Austin Papers," 2:166–67.

44. Eugene C. Barker, "The Career and Character of Stephen F. Austin," p. 15; and Austin to W. C. Carr, March 4, 1829, "Austin Papers," 2:178.

cultural journals after about 1850. Farmers and planters beautified homes and rural places by planting gardens with ornamental flowers and shrubs.[45]

Austin's ideal home reflected the best qualities of rural life, symbolizing forethought, diligence, and perseverance. But the physical manifestation of his goal—an agricultural society in Texas—was spoiled, he said, by that damnable "mania for speculation" to which Americans, not the Swiss or Germans, were peculiarly vulnerable. Any form of land dispute and speculation disturbed him. As self-proclaimed arbitrator and peacemaker, he felt threatened by lawyers, believing that they manipulated and dispossessed others and created, not relieved, tension and strife.[46]

Although Austin never had occasion to reap the "harvest," he never doubted the value of his efforts. In January, 1836, he declared that "a new republic is about to rear its independent banner over a country but lately a wilderness." Later in the same year he considered that "the foundation is laid . . . Texas is fully redeemed from the wilderness, and its independence is virtually achieved—this I call the *foundation.*"[47]

The "foundation" was human power over the wilderness. His colonists had pitted themselves against and vanquished primeval chaos and disorder; and in the tradition of his Puritan forebears, Austin imbued the act of settlement with ritual significance. Clearing the land and sowing crops were activities designed to redeem savage places from powers of evil and secure them for a community of Texans who, by asserting their dominance, demonstrated faith, zeal, and an elect status.

Austin became more sanguine about the character of the colonists he knew as time passed, for many of them were his people, and his agreement with his family of Texans was to deliver them into a promised land. Tribulations, in a sense, purified his soul by forcing a "leap of faith" toward a Texas-to-be. *Empresario* Austin believed he had a calling: he was to redeem Texas. This mission burned in his mind, becoming incandescent as he threw himself into his work. Certainly there were times of doubt. Imprisonment in Mexico in 1834 was an ordeal that left him "desolate—almost destitute of friends and money . . .

---

45. Stephen F. Austin to Mary Holley, January 14, 1832, "Austin Papers," 2:737; and December 29, 1831, 2:729.

46. Stephen F. Austin to Thomas F. Leaming, June 14, 1830, "Austin Papers," 2:415.

47. Stephen F. Austin to Mary Holley, January 7, 1836, "Austin Papers," 3:301; and Austin to W. S. Archer, August 15, 1836, "Austin Papers," 3:415.

amidst foes who are active to destroy me and forgotten at home by those I have faithfully labored to serve."[48] This "dark night of the soul," however, did not destroy his spiritual estate. Austin remained convinced of his Covenant, counterbalancing physical hardship with faith. His faith, which remained with him on his deathbed, was that his mission, the secular manifestation of spiritual selection, was accomplished.

48. Austin to James W. Breedlove, October 12, 1829, "Austin Papers," 2:268; and Austin to Samuel H. Williams, October 6, 1834, "Austin Papers," 3:7.

3. Wilderness Celebration: Making a Home in Texas

By means of steady, persistent attention to agriculture, colonists established new homes in the different land grants. They pushed out the frontier from outposts that Austin, DeWitt, and other *empresarios* established in the river valleys. Initial efforts concentrated in the undulating or rolling prairie zone behind the coast. But settlement soon extended toward the Gulf shore in the lower Brazos River Valley around Brazoria and along the lower reaches of the Guadalupe River. The tempo of agricultural expansion, geared to cotton, sugarcane, and corn, accelerated as people flocked into Texas after the Revolution. The face of the land changed as the area under cultivation grew, most notably in the old Mexican Department of Nacogdoches, between the Trinity and the Sabine rivers, and in the Department of Brazos, the center of Austin's initial colony.

As the wilderness retreated, its image changed in several significant ways. The wild fauna and flora that had once symbolized the land's aboriginal hostility were seen as advantageous. Native wildlife became an important source of food and provided fun and excitement from hunting, thereby making frontier conditions appear less oppressive. Male settlers talked incessantly about tracking and killing animals. Practicing hunting skills helped them to solidify personal bonds and to strengthen community solidarity.

Settlers also changed the negative image of wilderness by accentuating certain attractive features of Texas. In praising the beauties of nature, they felt, to some degree, less overwhelmed by feelings of isolation and loneliness. For example, people often wrote glowingly about certain times of the year, usually spring, when Texas looked its best. They expressed joy in being enveloped by the beautiful earth, participating in that bounteous and vibrant cycle of life. They admired beautiful scenery, the land's burgeoning fertility, and spoke enthusiastically of views, particularly of settlements that, from a distance, appeared to be part of the wild landscape. They made it clear that civilization was "fitting in" with the natural conditions of beautiful Texas and that a certain reciprocity existed between man and nature—a relationship of cooperation, not competition. After a wearying journey, the sight of San Antonio, New Braunfels, or Austin, usually lifted a traveler's spirits. Feeling secure on the outskirts of such urban places, people would pause and admire panoramas that combined the best handiwork of man and nature.

A third method of making the adjustment to strange and wild Texas was simply to make it appear like home. Accounts by Hispanic, American, and foreign authors abound in references to landscapes that reminded the writer of a homeland in Spain, England, Germany, Norway, or elsewhere, or one that resembled other regions in the United States. Many travelers and settlers derived comfort from the look of the land; a view of distant hills, the prospect of a river valley, or that special juxtaposition of woodland and prairie, conjured up images of other familiar places that were often hundreds, or perhaps thousands, of miles away. Such emphasis on visual similarities served, at least in the mind, to diminish the sense of loss that the journey had created. By emphasizing the familiar look of the land, not only actual distances seemed less, but the landscape of the past was linked to that of the present; there existed a continuity with lived experience between what had been and what was now. Such similarities in environmental images suggested to newcomers that they would be able to cope with the new reality because it was, reassuringly, not so different from the old.

Special events, such as encounters with wild animals, also endeared early Texas to people. These highly impressionistic experiences helped to attenuate the harshness of the frontier as individuals grew impressed and fascinated by unfamiliar flora and fauna. Such experiences kindled enthusiasm for places, making the experience of the Texas wilderness appear worthwhile.

Finally, some folk simply denied that Texas was a wilderness at all. Promoters and speculators, as we shall see in the next chapter, extolled Texas as a garden, not as a wilderness. Proponents of this viewpoint argued that all new settlers had to do was to pick over "the condiments" provided by nature's garden, which could then be tended and improved. By cultivating new plants and animals that suited economic and aesthetic needs, new settlers would flourish.

Abundant Wildlife for Recreation and Hunting

The appearance and habits of animals have kindled mankind's curiosity and imagination and have reassured us about nature's fecundity and goodness. People have greeted birds especially as faithful messengers of the seasons; they have wondered about their migrations and mysterious powers of flight. In boundless action "birds diversify the still landscape with the most lively motion and beautiful association," exclaimed an American ornithologist, Thomas Nuttall. Many of Nuttall's nineteenth-century colleagues noted that many feathered species assisted farmers by ridding fields of noxious insects. Scientists and artists described their odd shapes, colors, and song. Poets and nature writers were delighted by "conjugal fidelity and parental affection" of breeding birds, which exemplified civilized behavior and provided lessons for children.[1]

Texas residents, like others throughout the nation, were impressed by the large variety of birds, making particular note of the most useful, unusual, and beautiful species. Pelicans proved especially interesting to the thousands of foreign immigrants who landed in Galveston. A nesting colony of these odd-looking birds close to the harbor drew innumerable remarks.

Englishwoman Matilda Houstoun witnessed "an immense flight of hummingbirds," which do not live in Europe, as they arrived suddenly in Galveston in March, 1844. She found them fascinating and kept a few alive for several days by providing them with bread soaked in honey. Gazetteers and emigrant guides paid attention to oddities such as pelicans and hummingbirds, but also stressed the benefits of the insect-eating proclivities of wrens, flycatchers, and martins.[2]

Some birds reassured people who were lost or felt isolated in the wilds. In late summer, 1841, George Wilkins Kendall, a member of the

1. Thomas Nuttall, *A Manual of the Ornithology of the United States and Canada,* 1:1, 9.
2. Matilda Charlotte F. Houstoun, *Texas and the Gulf of Mexico,* p. 246.

ill-fated Santa Fe expedition, which had become thoroughly disoriented in West Texas, awoke to the "warbling of innumerable singing-birds." He recognized the notes of several species and believed that their singing indicated that a settlement was nearby. Though these songs kindled memories of his home, they turned out to be "fallacious promises," for he found no signs of settlement.[3] In the same decade at another place in West Texas, song and a sudden increase in bird numbers suggested that water was at hand. In this case, the indication proved true and the Pecos River, for which people had been searching, was discovered.[4]

Tradition correctly held that as clearings for agriculture became more numerous, the character of a region's birdlife changed. Smaller birds, especially insectivorous species, seemed actually to seek out the companionship of farmers; other species found farms good places to filch corn and fruit. The swallow was one of the "confiding" birds that people admired, although a few city residents damned cliff swallows for daubing courthouses and other buildings with mud nests. One was not supposed to molest the nests of barn swallows, fixed to the wooden rafters, because this friendly bird brought cheer and vitality to settled places.[5]

Andrew Muir's early book about Texas singled out the feisty mockingbird as another pleasing species, although it had a penchant for ripe fruit. This publication expressed disappointment about what was incorrectly reported as a small number of bird varieties, but the mocker, which possessed "great powers of buffoonery, versatility, and . . . coquetry," provided some compensation.[6]

Other writers also liked the "mischievous" mockingbird. "No other bird is so well protected by sentiment," declared Ralph A. Selle, who discovered in the "rapture of the woodland minstrel" a means for "lifting life's burdens." This competitor of the hermit thrush for the title of "American nightingale" thrived in Texas. Naturalist Roy Bedichek believed that the brush country between Hebbronville and the Rio Grande held more mockingbirds than anywhere else in the Southwest. He derived great pleasure from listening to the nocturnal lyrics of what

3. George Kendall, *Across the Great Southwestern Prairies*, 1:216.

4. Benjamin B. Harris, *The Gila Trail: Texas Argonauts and the California Gold Rush*, p. 44.

5. *Austin Daily Statesman*, April 10, 1883, recommended turning on water hoses to rid the courthouses of "these little pests"; see also A. E. Schutze, *The Summer Birds of Central Texas*, p. 21.

6. Samuel B. Buckley, *Second Annual Report of the Geological and Agricultural Survey of Texas*, p. 92; and Andrew F. Muir, ed., *Texas in 1837*, p. 126.

became Texas' state bird. One would commence to sing, others would join it, and together they would fill the moonlight air with melody, he noted. Doubtless, many Texas settlers before Bedichek's time received similar pleasure as they camped out in wild country, listening to "el troubador" perform his "poor man's symphony."[7]

Other animals offered similar comfort and that sense of well-being to early Texans, and the sheer abundance of many of them, specifically mammals and birds, impressed people. The unhealthful reputation of the Gulf Coast, for example, was compensated for to some degree in winter when the vast lowland hosted huge flocks of migratory birds. Englishman William Bollaert referred to Galveston Bay in the mid-1840s as a "great nation of geese."[8] Mary Austin Holley, who visited the coast near the Brazos River estuary, noted that, in season "large and almost innumerable" flocks of waterfowl grew so plentiful that "a single shot [would] often provide a meal for twenty persons." So populous was this goose "nation" that another source in the 1830s reported that the clamor of waterfowl could "be heard several miles." Additional chevrons of cranes and pelicans, together with shorebirds, hawks, eagles, wild turkeys, and smaller species, made the unsettled Gulf Coast a paradise for hunters. Conditions were best when a fresh wind blew or after a good chill had checked mosquitoes. Hunters, however, needed to be well acquainted with the marsh, swamp, and bay geography to navigate successfully. It was easy for someone unfamiliar with the open lowland to become lost in such a huge, remote, and swampy region.[9]

Almost fifty years later, conditions remained much the same on the lowland around Goliad, where one early pioneer remembered that wild game was so plentiful that it was "almost a nuisance." Animals became companions for newcomer John W. Lockhart, who headed across dismal, rain-sodden coast prairies between Houston and Washington-on-the-Brazos. Deer, turkeys, and other animals proved "comparatively gentle and easy to approach," said teenager Lockhart, who was comforted by these encounters on an otherwise depressing journey in 1840.[10]

In the early days when the Santa Fe Expedition was heading north

---

7. Ralph A. Selle, *El Jardin: Birds Sing in Texas*, pp. 14, 9, 10; and Roy Bedichek, *Adventures with a Texas Naturalist*, pp. 263–64.
8. W. Eugene Hollon and Ruth L. Butler, eds., *William Bollaert's Texas*, p. 317.
9. Mary Austin Holley, *Texas*, p. 100; and *A Visit to Texas*, p. 92.
10. James T. Johnson "Hardships of a Cowboy's Life in the Early Days of Texas," p. 762; and Jonnie L. Wallis, *Sixty Years on the Brazos: The Life and Letters of Dr. John Washington Lockhart*, p. 10.

from Austin, George Kendall noted how beautiful the surrounding countryside looked. Grapes festooned woodlands along the Brazos River and honey dripped "in almost every hollow tree." Adjacent prairies "teemed with every species of game," including wild turkeys, deer, and bears. The first glimpse of bison made the expedition's column erupt as every man grabbed a firearm and chased after the "lumbering haystacks." Such ebullience and optimism did not last. When game grew scarce, Kendall saw how men's spirits flagged as they grew moody and disconsolate; chasing animals for fun was a lingering memory — like a mirage in the West Texas plains. The expedition faced starvation, and they ate almost anything they could catch.[11]

Josiah Gregg was an expert plainsman in the 1830s. He also recognized that day-to-day travel grew tedious across these regions where the landscape resembled a wide ocean. He experienced the fears and tensions of the plains as violent storms blasted travelers, or bands of unpredictable Indians suddenly appeared. Gregg and others grew frustrated by mirages of lakes in this "Great American Desert," and by the plagues of insects that tormented man and beast. His journal reveals the value of encounters with wildlife in such inhospitable conditions. Wild animals were meat for hungry travelers who raced off to chase bison; but more important, the grace and beauty of antelope, deer, or mustangs buoyed people's jaded spirits, and many even grew curious enough to study the bustling ways of barking prairie dogs.

Wildlife offered Gregg more intangible satisfaction than simply meeting material needs. He was, for example, enchanted by the approaches to the Canadian River marked by fringes of timber on wetter soils, where "little herds of buffalo that were scattered about in fantastic groups imparted a degree of life and picturesqueness to the scene, which was truly delightful to contemplate." This was a stylized way of looking at potential quarry. He was pleased by the composition and aspect of the "canvas" that he stood back from in exerting his control. But he had no real commitment to his subject. Although condemning the excessive slaughter of bison and expressing remorse for the part he had played in such killing, Gregg excused the butchery by explaining just how contagious "buffalo fever" was. Hunting such big game mammals made human life exciting and different on the plains.[12]

The spectacle of large numbers of wild animals, like bison, captured

11. Kendall, *Across the Great Southwestern Prairies*, 1:109, passim.
12. Josiah Gregg, *The Commerce of the Prairies*, pp. 59, 89, 187, 189, 196, 317, passim.

people's imaginations and diverted attention from monotonous travel or difficult and unpleasant situations. The color, sounds, movements, and activities of birds and mammals exhilarated some folk, who grew curious about learning more, although others remained quite unmoved. These wonders of nature most often impressed foreign visitors, who were struck by the sheer numbers, never before having witnessed so many animals together. Native-born settlers and old-timers tended to shrug off such aggregations or took them for granted. To such laconic residents, herds of bison or antelope filling horizons, or bird flocks darkening skies, were a regular occurrence. The interior west teemed with life. Both residents and visitors, however, could agree on one point—their love for hunting. "Let no able bodied man emigrating to Texas neglect to provide himself with a good rifle or musket and at least one hundred rounds of ammunition," charged *The [Columbia] Telegraph* on May 2, 1837. Texas was famous for game animals. Men killed mammals and birds to feed their families and to barter or sell. And they gained enormous enjoyment from doing so; it was an escape from hard, often tedious, routines.

Settlers ran their hounds after bears; they set out live animals as decoys, and "jump shot" ducks. They practiced "shining," that is, hunting at night with a fire pan. They tracked down predators, lured turkeys close, and used greyhounds to run down deer, testing the endurance of both dogs and accompanying horses. "We did not kill for lust's sake, but for sport's sake," claimed one man. There was no point in killing large numbers; it was too easy. There was skill, however, in choosing the biggest buck and in having "contests to see who could kill at the greatest distance and with the cleanest shot." Such exploits, like mounting wild mustangs to break them, or being injured by the animal as it reared up and perhaps somersaulted backward, furnished enormous excitement, fun, and camaraderie to males on the frontier.[13]

I have published details of these recreational activities elsewhere; it is sufficient to record here that the wilderness experience provided opportunities to hone outdoor skills. Men enjoyed hunting for meat, skins, or feathers. But they loved the competition of woodcraft and marksmanship even more and taught eager youngsters how to identify, track, and kill the great variety of wild animals that inhabited early Texas. The wilderness was full of such opportunities.[14]

13. John T. Allen, *Early Pioneer Days in Texas*, pp. 30–31.
14. See Robin W. Doughty, *Wildlife and Man in Texas: Environmental Change and Conservation*, pp. 79–95.

"Beautiful" Texas Wilderness

Mexican official José María Sánchez, who accompanied Gen. Manuel de Terán and Jean Berlandier on a fact-finding tour of Texas, disliked San Felipe. In April, 1828, the settlement consisted of forty or fifty houses located on the west bank of the Brazos River. One of the two stores furnished the population of about two hundred with whisky, rum, sugar, and coffee; the other sold rice, flour, lard, and cheap cloth. Sánchez despised the place as shoddy and unkempt and found its American residents ill-mannered and indolent. He did not like the atmosphere; he sensed that trouble was brewing. A terrible storm added to his unhappiness. Bottomlands flooded and mosquito bites inflamed and bloodied human faces. The whole character of the land, which had earlier seemed so beautiful, especially the prairies around San Antonio, was reflected in the niggardliness of Jared Groce and his plantation, where, according to Sánchez, his party received a surprisingly inhospitable welcome.[15]

Between San Felipe and their destination, Nacogdoches, conditions further deteriorated. People were prostrated by sickness, heat, thirst, poor food, flooded tracks, and omnipresent, hellish insects. But suddenly, toward the end of his trek, Sánchez entered a clearing and immediately his spirits soared. The interminable woods of East Texas, where one felt trapped by a screen of damp foliage, had ended—for a space, at least. Finding a clearing purged his mind of that peculiar sense of confinement. "There is nothing," he wrote, "that affords the traveler in these solitary regions greater joy than the sight of a plain after coming out of the long, endless thick woods."

Sánchez withstood an unusually bad journey, but his comment demonstrated a common view in Texas, particularly for Mexicans, who were used to more open country. Generally, people favored the more open interior or rolling zone that lay between San Antonio and the Trinity River and spread northward to the Red River boundary. Passage through this area was easier and travelers enjoyed its "parkland" aspects, the pine and oak woods intermixed with grass-filled prairies. Stephen F. Austin planted his colony in this attractive ecotone between dense woodland and interior zone woodland and prairies. The tree canopy grew more extensive as one progressed east of the Brazos River Valley, and Sánchez

15. José María Sánchez, "A Trip to Texas in 1828," *Southwestern Historical Quarterly* 29 (1926): 249–88, especially pp. 271–72.

felt stifled by it. The prairies became larger, exposed, and more forbidding as one traveled west. Sánchez decribed the "desolate air" of treeless Laredo and its environs. But between the Balcones Escarpment and the Brazos and Trinity rivers was a fine country, which merged with the piney woods of Louisiana in the east and the grass-filled coastal lowlands in the south.[16]

This rolling prairie zone receives praise again and again in early comments about Texas because, as architecture scholar Christian Norberg-Schulz points out, it provides a landscape on a human scale. People discovered that the piney woods closed off the landscape, shutting out the sky, making the traditional "Nordic" landscape — a natural place to be "opened up" by felling the dense growth of woody vegetation. Similarly, many folk were intimidated by the wide plains, whose skyvault dominated the landscape, making it appear timeless, beyond human scale and measure. The middle ground between these two environments was that special juxtaposition of wood and prairie, earth and sky, that attracted human occupation. The idea of a natural garden focused on such a region, which reassured British travelers in particular that such a place already existed in the Texas wilds.

William Kennedy, whose *Texas* received important notice in the 1840s, admired the rolling prairies, principally because of the land's intrinsic beauty and fertility. Feelings of "lonesomeness" in the wilderness were dispelled by nature "embellished by the hand of art," he said. Fragile, delicate flowers, symmetric groves of trees, colorful birds, and warm sunlight made it possible to imagine that "such scenery had been created to gratify the refined taste of civilised man." It appeared that the country homes of English aristocrats already existed in Texas: "the lawn, the avenue, the grove, the copse, which are there produced by art, are here produced by nature," Kennedy remarked. In this sense, lands in Texas satisfied contemporary norms of landscape taste; Texas was, in large part, one enormous landscape garden.[17]

The prospect of deer bounding across sunlit openings or browsing quietly along a line of bushes fit this aesthetic mode perfectly. Add plaintive calls from quail or mourning doves, and the chattering of graceful scissor-tailed flycatchers, euphemistically called birds of para-

---

16. Ibid., p. 277.

17. See Christian Norberg-Schulz, *Genius Loci: Toward a Phenomenology of Architecture;* and William Kennedy, *Texas: The Rise, Progress, and Prospects of the Republic of Texas,* p. 106.

dise, to subtle perfumes from spring flowers, and the idyll was complete. All that was lacking was "massy architecture, and the distant view of villages," but settlements were on their way.[18]

One need not reject such elaborate descriptions of the countryside, and there are many of them, as mere hyperbole. People read them and reacted favorably to the images they conveyed. Promotional literature is replete with narratives that eulogized beautiful scenes and blue skies; it was the images that they conveyed, rather than the reality that they disguised, that are important. Potential settlers grabbed at these visions. Such picturesque images of Texas attracted them while assuring residents that the frontier wilderness was in many ways pleasing, too.

Most accounts made spring the finest season. Easterner Frederick Law Olmsted, who made many scathing remarks about Texas, fairly babbled with delight about springtime. "The beauty of the spring-prairies has never been and never will be expressed. It is inexpressible"; a "genial" sun, fresh, moistened sod, and flowers softened his heart. New plants, insects, parent mammals with young, and nesting birds showed off a pristine Texas, making life invigorating, even in relatively inhospitable places. The Gulf Coast prairie, where "the mind feels a kind of surprise at finding that the senses are almost useless where there is so little to give them exercise," looked its best in early spring.[19]

Sailing upstream to Brazoria, one author characterized the riparian prairie as " a smooth shaven lawn, or a vast sheet of velvet," where deer, cattle, and flocks of birds added scale and perspective. But flowers blanketing the grassland drew the most appreciation. Acres upon acres of wild flowers overpowered visitors with colors and scents. One traveler became giddy from looking closely at flowers spread in "concentric zones of the brightest yellow, red and blue in striking contrasts . . . a vast garden richly stocked with the finest plants." This colorful quilt extended to the horizon.[20]

In a paper entitled "Observations on the Geography of Texas" presented to the Royal Geographical Society in London in 1850, Bollaert wrote admiringly of the Texas prairie, noting "its verdure and flowers," which in spring were "in full bloom, filling the air with fragrance." In summer, the same land took on a golden hue as sun-ripe grasses waved

18. Kennedy, *Texas*, p. 106.

19. Frederick Law Olmsted, *A Journey through Texas*, p. 233; and *A Visit to Texas*, p. 19.

20. *A Visit to Texas*, pp. 18, 187.

in the breeze. As the year wore on, the same prairie turned "variegated, rich, and glowing." Bollaert took a keen interest in prairie flowers and in the many butterflies they attracted. Such rhapsodic descriptions helped to dispel popular fears about miasmatic chills and fevers in that flat country that one contemporary argued was "too much infested with alligators, moccason snakes and moschetoes."[21]

Many authors, however, made sure that readers had their feet squarely on the ground concerning the realities of living in Texas. Some of them had difficulties in describing the coastal prairies, specifically in conveying that such an "extent of flatness exists on this terrestrial clod." The mind will expand, they declared, in keeping with its surroundings and become filled with wonder and awe after contact with the coastal lowland. "Moccasons and moschetoes" or not, some folk knew that the "vast ocean of dry land," or, more specifically, "one great, Atlantic of land," as a Welsh immigrant put it, existed under a bluer, clearer, and purer sky than anywhere else. Traversing that prairie region could be a mystical experience, until the smell of a dismembered hog on the camp fire reminded one of corporeal necessities.[22]

Other open, flat lands—the Plains—were more difficult to beautify, although several people suggested images that made their wild qualities appear more palatable. In a useful overview, *The West as Romantic Horizon*, William H. Goetzmann and Joseph C. Porter have a place for Texas. West Texas, with neighboring regions, was a zone people traversed to get somewhere else. The Canadian River, slashing from west to east in the upper Panhandle, offered a passageway for Josiah Gregg and other traders between Missouri and Santa Fe. Austin and subsequent entrepreneurs argued that goods from the Rockies could find an outlet through Galveston after explorers and pathfinders had secured a trail from West Texas. Until the post–Civil War cattle boom, most people perceived the High Plains as home for bison, antelope, mule deer, and, of course, Indians. One did not venture too far into that huge, empty region, unless it was for purposes of establishing a fort or banding together in an emigrant train for the long trek to California.

The idea of "romantic horizon" was, therefore, one method of chang-

21. William Bollaert, "Observations on the Geography of Texas," *Journal of the Royal Geographical Society* 20 (1850): 113–35; quotations, p. 119; and Amos A. Parker, *Trip to the West and Texas*, p. 170.

22. Alexander E. Sweet and J. Amory Knox, *On a Mexican Mustang, through Texas, from the Gulf to the Rio Grande*, p. 68; and Alan Conway, ed., *The Welsh in America*, p. 15.

ing the negative feelings toward the clearly inhospitable plains, and it was an idea that would not have occurred a century earlier. Military officer Richard Irving Dodge recoiled in shock after his first glimpse of that vast country, but his surprise turned to awe over "the magnificence of being" in an environment that brought out the "true grandeur of manhood." This "grandeur" meant knowing how to survive on the frontier, pitting oneself against primitive forces while participating in exploits, such as hunting, that called for daring and skill (and supplied food). It also meant placing a structure as an artist would around the subject so as to control it better.[23]

Others recognized or "framed" the plains as "sublime and beautiful" in accordance with contemporary artistic conventions. This image struck Kendall in late August, 1841, when he joined a small party to seek assistance for the disoriented Santa Fe expedition. Looking down from an eminence at the tiny white-topped wagons stationed beside silver waters, he described the scene: "Almost the whole valley was bordered by the yawning chasms that had impeded the progress of our waggons, now brought more plainly to view by the elevation upon which we stood, and the whole scene forcibly reminded me of one of Salvator Rosa's beautiful landscapes, framed with rough, gnarled, and unfinished oak."[24] One can picture the erudite journalist squinting at the scene as through a Lorrain glass to organize the picture that a landscape painter would put on canvas. It was a way of controlling the environment, staying above and outside it. It was this view, perhaps of Palo Duro Canyon, that remained with Kendall. Later, charming vistas of his new home in Texas in what became Kendall County pleased him also, but they probably never compared with that dramatic moment in the West Texas wilderness.

In the summer of 1852, another explorer, Randolph Barnes Marcy, a nationally recognized expert on the Southwest, ventured up the headwaters of the Red River. Military authorities had instructed him to examine the strategic value of the country and its potential for Indian settlement. Marcy was good at his job and he enjoyed it. On July 1, he approached what he thought was the source of the Red River along its Prairie Dog Town Fork in West Texas. The majestic scenery thrilled him. Stupendous escarpments of solid rock towered into fantastic shapes from the riverbed. They were "the grandest, most picturesque scenes that can

23. Richard Irving Dodge, *The Hunting Grounds of the Great West.*
24. Kendall, *Across the Great Southwestern Prairies,* 1:231.

48

be imagined," he exclaimed. Living rock was transformed into a feudal castle with giddy battlements; a colossal, lofty human figure emerged from another rock pinnacle—"designed and executed by the Almighty artist as the presiding genius of these dismal solitudes." Such analogies to man-made structures placed the observer above nature and in a superior position to it. The scenery exemplified the hand of God, the architect of the universe, who stamped in rude nature "its primeval type, its unreclaimed sublimity and wildness." Marcy discovered God in the unexplored land. Human endeavors in this isolated region appeared insignificant, but with God at their side, people could take hope because a higher force guided their destinies.[25]

Later, Marcy entered a valley, "one of the most beautiful and romantic that I have ever seen," east of the Wichita Mountains and north of the Red River. A stream coursed through the three-mile-wide valley, cascading among rocks flanked by pecan, ash, elm, and post oak trees. Red cedar crowned the hills. Only pesky insects broke the repose of the scene. A lone bull bison, symbol of wild America, completed the picture of perfect primitive innocence. This allegory of nature's relationship to man treated landscape as a spectacle for wonder and contemplation. Marcy emphasized the dramatic qualities in the plains environment. The setting and its actors—beasts or aboriginals—were perceived as an inspiring and comforting manifestation of God's handiwork, a grand design created for the benefit of cultured and spiritually perceptive minds.[26]

Civilized man had a place on the frontier as well. William Parker, who rode with Marcy across North Texas, noted as they broke camp that someone had started a prairie fire. The plume of fierce flames and smoke composed the "striking picture of the sublime," he said. The distant column of smoke on one side was balanced with a similar column of cloud on the other, with the wilderness in between.[27]

Such pious and romanticized images helped to lessen the tensions of life, at least for a select group, in a remote, difficult region. Natural wildness, it was argued, inspired observers and provided them with opportunities for heroic deeds—Kendall's, for example. Such heroes braved the frontier to explore, survey, or barter with Indians. They informed

25. United States, War Department, *Adventure on Red River,* p. 91.
26. Ibid., p. 114.
27. William B. Parker, *Notes Taken during the Expedition Commanded by Captain R. B. Marcy,* p. 88.

others in settled places about the resources and the lay of distant lands, and they made suggestions about how to read new country and how to anticipate and cope with difficult conditions. In *The Prairie Traveller*, for instance, Randolph Marcy made suggestions about travel routes in the west, appropriate food, clothing, and campsites. He advised readers about Indian customs and ways to hunt game. In sum, he wrote down everything a traveler needed to know about surviving on the open plains. The adventures inspired writings tempered with practical advice and helped to diminish the "darkness" of the wilderness.[28] The successors to the frontiersmen, the stockmen, who were also epic figures as cowboys, assumed the less adventurous but still romantic role of settling the southwestern frontier with their alien livestock.

Wilderness as Home

In the introduction to his monumental work *Cosmos,* explorer-scientist Alexander von Humboldt examined human fears about unfamiliar regions and attempted to explain them. Von Humboldt, genius and precursor to Charles Darwin, explored widely in Latin America in the early 1800s. In his discussion of New Spain, or Mexico, he likened El Paso to Spain's Andalusia. Such analogies, he argued, were perfectly normal. "The flexibility of our nature fits us to receive new impressions," the scientist said, so that we may turn them, albeit gradually, into feelings that attach us to a new home. One way of creating a sense of attachment was to give common names to new, unknown organisms, thereby turning strange objects into likenesses of well-recognized ones. "Yet fearful, as it were, of breaking links of association that bind him to the home of the childhood, the colonist applies to some few plants in a far-distant clime the name he had been familiar with in his native land," concluded von Humboldt.[29]

American bird names such as "robin," "flycatcher," and "blackbird" stem from colonial times when early writers labeled specimens from their superficial resemblance to European birds. In Texas and elsewhere in the South, the common name "crow-blackbird" referred to grackles,

28. Randolph B. Marcy, *The Prairie Traveller.*
29. Alexander von Humboldt, *Cosmos: A Sketch of a Physical Description of the Universe,* introduction.

which had dark coloration and were intermediate in size between the European carrion crow and the blackbird, a member of the thrush family. Similarly, the colorful scissor-tailed flycatcher, with its long, forked tail, reminded people of illustrations of birds of paradise, which also sported long nuptial plumes. Polish peasants used the word *wilk,* meaning "wolf," for the coyote. They also transferred the word for the pine marten, "kuna" to the raccoon, which was unknown in their homeland. "Peach" lands referred to soils on which a native indicator plant grew, whose leaves, according to Holley, tasted like a peach-stone kernel. What von Humboldt argued was true: colonists searched for the "affinity existing among all forms of organic life," a habit that enhanced the feeling of at-homeness in new environments, though they frequently perceived greater similarity than existed in reality.[30] Stressing the variety of wildlife and beauties of nature, as we have seen, helped settlers to acclimate to wild lands. Together, these more pleasant aspects of the frontier experience made it appear more like a "home," as important, in time, as the homes they had left behind.

The environmental image of home in early Texas was promulgated in two ways. First, widely read authors, promoters, and visitors discovered in different places at various times landscapes that reminded them of the "old country" in Western Europe or in other states or regions of North America. Second, colonists who had made the journey and established themselves mailed so-called America letters back to friends and relatives in distant countries. They shared experiences with eager readers, and their letters inspired emigration. Foreign travelers and pioneers often compared new environments with their regions of origin, so that, to some, Central Texas resembled Germany's Rhineland; to others, England's Somerset or Kent. Such images of homeland transplanted made the wild character and strangeness of Texas appear less hostile and forbidding.

In the period between first settlement and the Civil War, the appearance of Texas reminded many newcomers of places they had left behind. Kennedy, as we have noted, praised the parklike qualities of the interior rolling region. Deer constantly crossed the traveler's path or grazed "on the flowery prairies, heightening the resemblance of those wooded meadows, to the parks of the British aristocracy." A truer member of Britain's aristocracy, Amelia Matilda Murray, toured the area of

30. Elsa G. Allen, *The History of American Ornithology before Audubon;* and Holley, *Texas,* pp. 50–51.

Austin's first grant in 1855. Lady-in-waiting to Her Majesty Queen Victoria, this gentlewoman turned in a gritty performance for a frontier "greenhorn." Her curiosity carried her on horseback deep into the solitude of the Brazos Valley. The spry sixty-year-old Lady Amelia took a keen interest in natural history; she inquired about the plants, made pets of horned frogs, and was so favorably impressed that she concluded that the pattern of timber and openings resembled "Somersetshire, Kent, and Windsor Forest by turns." Her Majesty doubtless listened with amusement to the elderly lady's stories about roughing it on the Texas frontier.[31]

Visitor Ferdinand von Roemer compared Texas with Germany. He judged for example, that the Adelsverein's Nassau Plantation near Industry looked like "a certain region of the Rhine." Showing a good eye for detail, the scientist noted that two kinds of stone made up San Antonio's Mission San José. One of them "is a light, porous, tufaceous limestone or travertine, which is also found in many parts of Germany, as for example on the area of the Leine Valley in the vicinity of Goettingen."[32]

Birds and trees also impressed Roemer. "The order of birds is also well represented in New Braunfels," he said. He missed the familiar nightingale and skylark, but was cheered by notes from the Texas mocker and redbird or cardinal. He argued, "If it should seem to the German immigrant in America that the woods are not populated with birds, especially song birds, as in the homeland, this is not the case. In the center of the vast German forests and uncultivated land, comparatively few song birds would also be found."[33]

Roemer subscribed to the belief that cultivation and settlements attracted birdlife: Texans had nothing for which to apologize. A German newcomer, said the European, would find "the forests of western Texas similar to those of his native country. He does not find any species of trees which appear foreign to him such as palms and the like." Humboldt's feelings of "affinity" were sure to grow as he and his companions recognized other familiar flora and fauna in Texas.[34]

Frederick Law Olmsted loved the "German qualities" of Texas. He thought that New Braunfels was a clean, neat, attractive, well-organized,

31. Kennedy, *Texas*, p. 123; and Marilyn M. Sibley, "The Queen's Lady in Texas," *East Texas Historical Journal* 6 (1968): 114.

32. Ferdinand von Roemer, *Texas: With Particular Reference to German Immigration and the Physical Appearance of the Country*, p. 128.

33. Ibid., pp. 140–41.

34. Ibid., p. 142.

and increasingly prosperous community in the early 1850s. The contrast between German settlements and the remainder of the state overwhelmed him. "I never in my life . . . met with such a sudden and complete transfer of associations," he exclaimed. In place of crude log walls stuffed with rags, Olmsted stayed in "one of these delightful little inns which the pedestrian who has tramped through the Rhine land will ever remember gratefully." In short, "we were in Germany!"[35]

Olmsted recognized other similarities, albeit faint ones, with New England and other places in the east. The city of Austin was a picturesque locality and reminded him of Washington, "*en petit,* seen through a reversed glass." He sneered at the "very remarkable" number of places for drinking and wagering in the city, and at the absence of a single bookstore. He thought that San Antonio was a remote outpost, but attractive, exuding an air of foreignness, like New Orleans. Its residents, however, tended toward idleness, alcoholism, and violence ("murders, from avarice or revenge, are common here"). Olmsted tended to withhold approval for people and places in non-German Texas.[36]

Other writers were more generous. David Woodman claimed in his *Guide to Texas Emigrants* (1835), written to promote land sales primarily in East Texas, that the rolling land dissected by the Trinity, San Jacinto, and Neches rivers resembled "that of New Jersey, and the lower counties of Pennsylvania and Delaware." It was, of course, agriculturally more productive. The Galveston Bay and Texas Land Company, for which Woodman probably worked, pushed hard to sell land early in the 1830s to satisfy backers in New York and Boston. This policy eschewed Austin's previous commitment to "silent" settlement by endeavoring to clarion the virtues of Texas to prospective settlers who could purchase thousands of acres of landscape for five cents an acre. Landscapes that reportedly looked like home to easterners and Europeans were part of this promotion.[37]

Promoters worked hard to attract foreigners. James Power appealed to Irish Catholics to settle his disputed land grant between the Lavaca and Nueces rivers near the coast. Power discovered landscapes from today's Eire in coastal Texas. Wexford in southeast Ireland sat on a bay just like Copano, which he expected to become an important port.

35. Olmsted, *Journey through Texas,* pp. 143–44.
36. Ibid., pp. 110–11, 150–59.
37. David Woodman, *Guide to Texas Emigrants,* p. 31.

Live Oak Peninsula, north of present-day Rockport, supposedly resembled the separation of Wexford Bay from St. George's Channel. This veritable home-away-from-home in Texas did not initially prosper. The first 350 or so immigrants braved a cholera epidemic, and later the Mexican Army destroyed their settlement of Refugio, the site of an abandoned mission, whose male population was also decimated in the Goliad Massacre.[38]

A different but complementary source for promoting Texas' similarities with other countries was "America letters," which immigrants wrote to friends and relatives, who passed them around and sometimes published them. Norwegian settlers around the area of present-day Dallas from the late 1840s provide one valuable source for comparisons between Europe and Texas. Carlton C. Qualey has pointed out that the "Norwegian-American community paid Texas attention out of all proportion to the actual numbers of settlers who made it their home." Three people, Cleng Peerson, Johan Reinert Reiersen, and Elise A. Waerenskjold are the reason. All three immigrants were well-respected, skillful communicators; Elise Waerenskjold, in particular, was an indefatigable correspondent for almost fifty years from her home on Four-Mile Prairie in Van Zandt and Kaufman counties.[39]

Cleng Peerson, the "vagabond-like Daniel Boone of Norwegian migration," traveled widely in the United States for many years to promote immigration, finally reaching Texas for the second time in 1849 and making it his home. Johan Reiersen founded the Norwegian colony at Brownsboro, in Henderson County, after casting about for suitable sites in midwestern states. He founded a magazine, *Norway and America,* which published information and opinions about emigration, in the same month (July, 1845) in which he settled in Texas. He grew to love Texas and unceasingly encouraged his countrymen to come to the new state. In 1852, Reiersen recommended an unsettled area about twenty miles east of Fort Worth. Its steep sandstone cliffs dominated small valleys filled with fine grass, clear water, and excellent soils. Oak, not pine, dominated the "mountain slopes"; however, he was prepared to stake his reputation on the region's value for incoming Norwegians.[40]

38. Hobart Huson, *The Refugio Colony and Texas Independence,* p. 2; and John B. Flannery, *The Irish Texans.*

39. Carlton C. Qualey, *Norwegian Settlement in the United States,* p. 198; Theodore C. Blegen, *Land of Their Choice,* p. 351.

40. Blegen, *Land of Their Choice,* p. 17 (quotation); Theodore C. Blegen, *Norwegian Migration to America: 1825–1860,* 1:182–84; and Lyder L. Unstad, "Norwegian Migration

Waerenskjold adopted Texas as her new home in 1847. A friend of Reiersen, she edited the second volume of his *Norway and America* and through her letters and articles made Texas appear close and familiar to many Norwegians. She made it clear that "every possible link with the beloved land of our birth is important and precious to us," and one of the key links was similarities in the appearance of the landscape. Reiersen noted that the area around Brownsboro looked like Norway. Waerenskjold concurred; Amli parishioners in Norway would view the same kind of hilly country with "high ridges and large pine woods." Woody vegetation invaded the prairies over the course of the next twenty-five years, however, and shrubs spread under the canopy of pines.[41]

Her home in the nearby community of Four-Mile Prairie, thirty-six miles from Brownsboro, resembled the openness of Denmark. She liked to be reminded of Norway, however, and thanked a correspondent in 1867 for photographs, asking whether it was "possible to get views of landscapes or are they expensive?" Such pictures of the old home were of great comfort.[42]

A major controversy was sparked when correspondence written by a Frenchman, Captain Tolmer, appeared in Norwegian newspapers. In ten letters to the *Journal des Debats* (about 1849), he lambasted Texas. Waerenskjold leaped to the state's defense. She rejected the accusation that the struggle between man and nature was both fierce and hazardous in Texas, arguing that "people have far less difficulty in Texas than in Norway." In Texas, a farmer needed to fence, plow, sow, and await harvest. Then the wheat "is simply placed on the ground and trampled out by horses or oxen." Grain would be lost in this slipshod way, but a thirty-bushel-per-acre yield from only four bushels of seed was possible. It was "above the average," and with care yields would be much higher, especially for rye, barley, and oats.

Waerenskjold also pointed out that wild animals posed few problems. Attacks on humans were exceedingly rare, and a person could "sleep quite securely, even though unarmed and far from people, whether it be on the prairie or in the woods." Chicken snakes, occasionally climbing into houses to hunt hen eggs "under the beds and up in the lofts," frightened but did not harm people. Most wild creatures were "more

---

to Texas: A Historic Resume with Four 'American Letters,'" *Southwestern Historical Quarterly* 43 (1939): 176–95, especially p. 192.
41. Blegen, *Land of Their Choice*, pp. 326, 335.
42. Ibid., p. 332.

amiable than those in Norway," she said; certainly nature was more fe-
cund, and people were friendly, helpful, equal, and free. Twenty-three
other settlers, including Cleng Peerson, joined Waerenskjold in condemning Tolmer's account.[43]

Waerenskjold paints a picture of nature cooperating with human activities that complements the idea that the settlement process completed
or crowned the physical environment. Other people like her argued that
houses, crops, fields, and other works of man harmonized with the
natural world. Cultural objects could be said to improve on nature by
mitigating disorder or disunity in the sense that Buffon had employed
the concept earlier; that is, human handiwork reflected man's steward-
ship over nature. People were the finishers of Creation. At the same
time, the existence of houses, fields, and other manifestations of human
presence reflected the sense of dwelling in the world. The engagement
of the environment on this basis gathered together physical objects, resources, and the cultural framework to produce the sense of place, reflecting a bond between man and landscape.

Abolitionist Benjamin Lundy looked out from a hill across a pano-
rama of woodland and clearings as he headed west for San Antonio in
the 1830s. This vegetation pattern extended "as far as the eye could reach,"
he said, "like a region thickly settled with farms and plantations. Houses
alone were wanting to perfect the resemblance."[44] This appealing image, created from the natural juxtaposition of plant cover, became even
more attractive when appropriate animals such as deer, turkeys, mustangs, or antelope were part of the scene. The presence of human habitations and clearings, whether natural or man-made, added picturesque
elements to the pastoral motif. But the presence of "farms and plantations" stood for more than visual reassurance; they also represented the
journey's end for the traveler: a refuge. Coming on settlements inhabited by one's fellows lifted a traveler's spirits and helped to allay fears
about distances by making them appear shorter. The loneliness and isolation of the frontier was dispelled when one passed through cleared
or settled areas.

Ferdinand von Roemer, the so-called father of Texas geology, spent
almost eighteen months in Texas in the mid-1840s, mainly in Central

43. C. A. Clausen, ed., *The Lady with the Pen*, pp. 28, 30, 38.
44. Benjamin Lundy, *The Life, Travels and Opinions of Benjamin Lundy, Including
His Journeys to Texas and Mexico*, p. 42.

Texas. In the summer of 1846 he journeyed north up the Brazos River into country where he fell ill and turned back to Austin—a three-day journey during which he came upon only three habitations. Finally, he returned to his lodgings in New Braunfels, confessing that "I greeted the sight of the Verein buildings, glittering in the sun, with joy, for several days prior to this I had had grave doubts whether I should ever see them again."[45]

Roemer, like others, felt most comfortable among fellow countrymen. He passed seventeen days slogging through sodden country on his initial trip from Houston to New Braunfels. He was forced to camp in the rain and cold on the community's outskirts when men refused to ferry him across the river at night. Knowledge that he was virtually within a stone's throw of shelter and comfort made his plight seem more acute. However, as soon as fellow Germans transported him to the settlement the next morning, the arduousness of his trek grew less disagreeable. His relief, he reported, "was greatly enhanced upon entering the principal street of New Braunfels where we saw German faces, German dress and, in general, signs of German manner of living."[46]

People of similar backgrounds and nationalities shared experiences in unfamiliar settings. Almost twenty years earlier, Mexican national José Sánchez was much relieved when he saw San Antonio. He entered the city after a ten-day winter journey from Laredo in much better weather than Roemer encountered. Fears about possible Comanche attacks, tempests, and embarking on such a long journey through uninhabited country subsided. The cluster of houses around Mission La Espada greeted him. "The sight of those dwellings brought forcefully to my mind that I was still living among my fellowmen," the weary traveler commented.[47]

Similar anxieties appear frequently in diaries and travel accounts. Settlements on the frontier were oases of security. As people passed along the rough tracks between them, navigating around swollen creeks or confusing landmarks, the nearer they believed their destinations to be, the higher their spirits soared. Some folk like Daniel Shipman did not appear to mind three or four days "without seeing the face of a human being." But on meeting up with others, travelers frequently banded

45. Roemer, *Texas*, p. 208.
46. Ibid., p. 90.
47. Sánchez, "A Trip to Texas," p. 257.

together. Indians, however, were not part of this camaraderie. Settlers and travelers treated them with circumspection, often refusing to camp in their vicinity.[48]

The settlement of Fort Mason, her journey's end, was a welcome relief for Eliza Johnston, who moved to Texas with her military officer husband in 1856. Her journal of the more than ten-week journey to a military post near the San Saba River on the eastern edge of the Hill Country vividly records her feelings of elation and despondence in trying circumstances. The reader can almost sense the pain of biting cold, bone-wearying fatigue, and her deep sorrow in burying in an unmarked grave the body of a young soldier who died of sickness. Others reciprocated her many small but thoughtful kindnesses with gifts of food. People did what they could for each other.

On January 13, Johnston looked across a beautiful winter scene. The booming void, dotted occasionally with trees, burned incandescently with greens and browns under a bright sun. "The scene had all the effect of a midsummer harvest, it was like a dream of August," she said, shivering with cold. The final day's move promised warmth and comfort in Forth Worth.[49]

On occasion, however, reassurance in the wilderness came not from scenery or the safety of nearby destinations, but from objects that today we call trifles. Mary J. Eubank, eldest daughter of Joseph Eubank (who invented an improvement for the cotton gin), accompanied her family from Kentucky to Texas in 1853. They crossed the Red River on the Fulton Road and headed for lands on the San Gabriel River in eastern Williamson County. Conditions deteriorated. Wagons became stuck, horses took sick, boatmen proved irascible, and "Pa has not yet found land to please him and he is very much discouraged," wrote twenty-one-year-old Mary. Two events, however, lifted her spirits. One was the pleasure of a candy stew after camp supper one evening; the other was a bar of soap that she purchased in Paris, Texas, "for thirty cents." Small items like candy and soap spelled relief from the grind of searching for good water, keeping dry, and feeding on wild game. Rather than being dour or insignificant moments, experiences like these made up the routines by which people located their own place in the world.[50]

48. Daniel Shipman, *Frontier Life: 58 Years in Texas,* p. 49.

49. Charles P. Roland and Richard C. Robbins, eds., "The Diary of Eliza (Mrs. Albert Sidney) Johnston," *Southwestern Historical Quarterly* 60 (1957): 463–500; quotation, p. 489.

50. W. C. Nunn, "A Journal of Our Trip to Texas, October 6, 1853, by Mary James Eubank," *Texana* 10 (1972): 30–44; quotation, p. 39.

Texas as a Special Place

A final way of turning back the negative influence of the wilderness involved experiences that revealed the character of a place. Sometimes, episodes that happened in a place proved so vivid or meaningful that they made living on the frontier seem worthwhile. Several striking instances occur in publications about Texas.

The first one involved Gideon Lincecum (1793–1874), for whom wilderness Texas was a special place. Lincecum was born in the backwoods of Georgia and learned outdoor skills, including medical lore and natural history, from friendly Indians. In 1835, he explored Texas with the idea of making it his home. Companions left him in the vicinity of Bastrop after he had decided to push deeper into south-central Texas. So, alone and for the most part avoiding habitations, this backwoodsman continued his exploration of the country.

In March, he left pioneer Jesse Burnam's home on the Colorado River and lived by catching fish and hunting waterfowl when deer were scarce. He stopped at a cabin on the south bank of the San Bernard, east of the Colorado River, then he decided to visit the seacoast, a dozen or so miles away. A local settler named Churchwell disliked the fierce Indians of the beach region and was unwilling to venture there. Around sunset, Lincecum came across hundreds of swans resting on coastal waters. Seemingly at a signal, the huge flock of birds took flight, swinging over the solitary human at a height of no more than thirty feet. It took the vast congregation of these graceful but gigantic birds several minutes to pass overhead, recalled Lincecum, and as they did so he grew numb from the concussion of their large wings, which "seemed to devitalize the air. My breathing was painfully oppressed while the living tornado passed over me," he exclaimed. He sank to earth exhausted, having witnessed "the flight of the southern division of American swans." This event eclipsed previous experiences of stampeding bisons, flights of wild pigeons, or galloping mustangs. His sudden encounter with whistling swans was that special moment that doubtless contributed to making his Texas home a unique place.[51]

Three years later, Mary Holley recorded a similarly remarkable experience near the San Bernard River along the coast. Her party camped on the San Bernard and feasted on roasted oysters. The next morning, in windy conditions, one of her companions set fire to the prairie,

---

51. Lois Wood Burkhalter, *Gideon Lincecum, 1793–1874: A Biography*, p. 40.

thereby forcing them to whip the horses into a furious gallop to out-pace the crackling flames. As night approached, a line of fire extended for eight or nine miles in one direction while the dashing surf presented a second spectacle and the golden sunset a third. Holley tarried as "the curling flames rose high making something like an arch over a gate-way." She passed through an opening in the flames. Inside, "a black carpet covered the surface far ahead and on either side were the lines of flame so that we were completely shut in by fire—whose weird and distant light served to make the darkness more visible." Truly, she said, it was a subject for a painter. "Never did I witness in the same scene, so many picturesque objects."[52]

Special experiences might concern animals. Ferdinand von Roemer was accompanying a gunsmith on a visit to a Caddo village north of Torrey Trading House in McClennan County near the Brazos River. On the way, Roemer came upon buffalo, which he "had long cherished the wish to see. . . . This desire had increased since I had seen so many tracks crossing our road the day before." Roemer exclaimed, "Now all of a sud-den a whole herd stood before us," and because of the wind's direction he was able to "examine their ungainly bodies and clumsy movements in a leisurely way." His longing to see bison was well satisfied. On that very special day, he saw herds of three thousand to four thousand head and worked within range of several animals but did not shoot. He was content just to observe wild bison, which had become increasingly scarce farther south. Roemer savored this event, which he had come so far to see.[53]

John Russell Bartlett had a similar experience with mustangs a few years later. In December, 1852, the boundary commissioner's party left the Rio Grande for Corpus Christi, crossing the grasslands of the South Texas Plain. After a week, Bartlett noted mustangs growing numerous. Wild horses came up to their camp and made mules restive. On De-cember 30, the commissioner again saw mustangs; they galloped at full speed, "presenting a beautiful spectacle as they stretched for a mile or more, with their long bushy tails streaming in the wind." And on the following day, Bartlett noticed that the whole horizon seemed to be moving "with long undulations, like the waves of the ocean." Through a telescope, Bartlett realized that the entire country was alive with mus-tangs, which were racing toward his party. As the lines of wild horses

52. Mary Austin Holley, *Mary Austin Holley: The Texas Diary, 1835–1838*, p. 64.
53. Roemer, *Texas*, pp. 191–200; quotation, p. 199.

began to swing past, one of the mule teams stampeded and took off after the wild bands. Teamsters quickly bunched the restive animals together so that only a few mules actually saw the wild horses. Bartlett dismounted and began to fire into oncoming bands. "The leader was turned," he said, "and the avalanche of wild animals swept by us like a tornado, much to our relief."[54]

This narrative, full of vigor and action, is unusual because on more than one occasion Bartlett reported that life on the plains tended to be extremely monotonous. There would be days when no birds were seen except omnipresent crows, which followed men to pick over campsites. Rabbits and wolves were the most frequent mammals in otherwise barren lands. This event with mustangs was, therefore, unusual, although the lower Nueces basin became famous for its wild horses.[55]

The bustle and excitement of such an encounter certainly made an excellent entry in the travelog. It was one of those remarkable events that gave a unique stamp to frontier Texas. After all, where else could one go to see the tornadoes of swans, mustangs, and prairies alive with bison or swept by enormous fires? Such spectacles may not have made life on the frontier simpler or easier, but they injected dramatic qualities that, for some, hepled to make life there meaningful and worthwhile.

54. John Russell Bartlett, *Personal Narrative of Explorations and Incidents in Texas, New Mexico, California, Sonora and Chihuahua,* 2:521–24; quotations, pp. 521, 522, 524.
55. Ibid., 2:555–56.

4. Nature's Bounties in Garden Texas

Gardens reflect environmental attitudes. The enclosed garden or cloister was a monastic institution wherein the dedicated individual meditated on human values within the security and serenity of a rural retreat. The garden spelled disengagement from the trials of secular life, particularly the tribulations of the city. It also represented the simpler environment to which humans returned to seek closer contact with nature. The migration of Europeans to America was conceived by many as the retreat to a pastoral ideal; it was "a symbolic movement toward a new, simpler, and happier way of life." The American South best represented this natural garden in which deputies of the English establishment promoted a planter economy. It was the good land figuratively flowing with milk and honey. The Republic of Texas fulfilled this image quite literally, as both cattle and wild bees abounded. Boosters saw Texas offering blandishments that could not fail to satisfy American and foreign settlers, and their rhetoric affirmed the need for pastoral felicity and personal satisfaction.[1]

But commentators emphasized those pastoral qualities of the Texas environment that spelled profit and progress. Theirs was a future Texas, one that required more and more hands to till the soil and embellish it with useful plants and animals. The image of this special, natural

1. Yi-Fu Tuan, *Topophilia: A Study of Environmental Perception, Attitudes, and Values*, p. 138; and Leo Marx, "Pastoral Ideals and City Troubles," p. 98.

place was not new; everyone recognized it. Annette Kolodny has likened the idea of the garden to the emblem of fecundity as a virgin or mistress in American experience. The virgin land awaited impregnation from the exertions of settlers; the beautiful woman was an emblem of nurturing and comfort and, as a helpless maiden, required care and attention. The garden image, like that of the wilderness, therefore, was derivative. In the Texas case, the term occurred in popular literature to signify the provision of material goods with little or no toil. Provision meant profit, getting more from the investment of time and labor than you put in. It was a capitalist garden, which meant agriculture for profit rather than agriculture as a way of life. At least, that is what so many promotional books and journal articles argued.[2]

One may say at the outset that Garden Texas was not intended primarily to be a Texas home, but a means to individual aggrandizement through land speculation and boosterism. This was scarcely the image that Austin had in mind in describing his "harvest" sequence. For Austin, the garden was a home in which Texans would discover the virtues of rural life. It was that Jeffersonian ideal of rural family farms in which American yeomen dedicated themselves to husbandry. But it was preempted by a progressive, more militant image in which urban growth and "civilization," expressed by an expansive industrial order, was a welcome addition. Whether it threatened the pastoral qualities of Garden Texas did not seem to matter. Many people spoke of the garden, therefore, from the perspective of "outside" promoter.

"Insider" resident views surface as well. Kolodny has also made the point that, although many women may have felt disenfranchised on the frontier, quite often they literally tended a garden around their dwellings—it was a garden within the Garden, a physical symbol expressing the full meaning of place and home as domestic space, not just a romantic pastoral retreat. Not every homekeeper took to garden tending, but a great many women decorated their places with ornamental flowers, shrubs, and herbs, making a mark of personal care and commitment on the land. Kolodny singles out Mary Austin Holley for promoting the sense of a domestic or "Social Eden" in Texas, the Anglo inhabitants of which formed an extended family under the patronage of her cousin Stephen F. Austin.[3]

2. Annette Kolodny, *The Lay of the Land.*
3. Annette Kolodny, *The Land before Her,* pp. xiii, 101–103.

Bounteous Texas

Two factors determined the quality of human life in Texas: climate, which affected health, and soils, which controlled the availability and variety of food. Climate and health were inseparable in literature from the 1830s, and favorable characterizations of both helped solidify the garden image. One of the most effective communicators about these two elements was Holley, whose Texas letters (1833) and *Texas* (1836) opened the era of Texas travel writing. Numerous authors depended both explicitly and surreptitiously on Holley's publications. Austin encouraged and helped her with both books.[4]

Holley and her successors repeatedly emphasized two outstanding qualities of the Texas climate: equability and salubrity. It was Eden-like, with a "perpetual summer," she argued. Cooling southeast breezes tempered the hottest months as the sun's heat on the flat, dry, coastal expanse pulled in air from the Gulf. North winds from November to March swept cold air over the plains, but sharp, moist, cold blasts from "northers" were short-lived. They served, Holley argued, "to purify the atmosphere," giving the climate a general "blandness" that enabled garden plants to survive even in winter.

Freed from extremes of heat and cold, equable weather also spelled healthfulness. Northers, sea breezes, dry summers, and a scarcity of overflow lands with their stagnant pools reportedly inhibited endemic diseases but did not eradicate miasmatic fevers. How, then, did Holley explain illness? She admitted that "sickness prevails to some extent," mainly because of woodlands. The presence of Spanish moss on trees, for instance, indicated unhealthy places; but she argued that a general absence of dense undergrowth in Texas forests made them far healthier than those in adjacent states. Geographical lore reckoned that the use of the axe permitted the sun's rays to penetrate the surface of cut-over woodlands, releasing pent-up gases. These vapors caused temporary "fever and ague bottom." Additionally, people believed it healthier to build cabins on drier prairies. In sum, healthfulness increased as surface moisture decreased, so that, according to Holley and other commentators, mainly dry summers and fewer swamps than in other places in the South helped to mitigate malarial complaints.[5]

4. Rebecca Smith Lee, *Mary Austin Holley: A Biography*, pp. 223–51, especially p. 231, passim.

5. Mary Austin Holley, *Texas*, pp. 40–46; and idem, *Texas: Observations, Historical, Geographical and Descriptive in a Series of Letters*, pp. 120–21.

Holley tried to deemphasize the disadvantages of Texas' weather and climate, but William Kennedy (1841) was more forthright. He admitted that the weather could be terrible. Floods, high winds, and chilling northers often occurred suddenly and unexpectedly, but compared with Louisiana and other places, Texas was a paradise. Again, like Holley and others, Kennedy's opinions were directed by the then current belief that wetlands were directly responsible for fevers: "Putrid swamps, the exhalations from which, under the rays of the burning sun, poison the atmosphere, and produce sickness and death," was his graphic comment. He agreed with Holley that the swamplands in Texas were not extensive, and those fevers that people associated with forest clearing were reportedly of the intermittent kind, diminishing as settlement expanded.[6]

Texas, concluded the Irishman, offered little encouragement "to the swarms of medical practitioners that yearly issue from the universities and colleges of Europe." Riparian woodlands near the coast proved the most testing environment, as trees attracted rain-filled clouds whose precipitation led to overflows. Elsewhere much more salubrious and beautiful landscapes existed. Away from the coast, he said, "no part of the globe is more friendly to the regular action of the human frame." And he considered nine-tenths of the Republic better than the most healthful regions of the United States.[7]

Texas soils proved generally good. Holley's customary hyperbole "challenged all other countries for a comparison, both as to quality and variety," including "clayey, sandy, pebbly, rocky, with all their intermixtures." Many authors echoed her sentiments about the physical geography. Initially, speculation existed about whether prairies were really suitable for cultivation, although pioneers planted crops on them. Holley skirted this issue, stating that prairie soils were well adapted for grazing, whereas alluvial soils on the coastal plain—the proverbial "peach and cane lands"—proved highly productive. These were chocolate-colored soils covered by thick cane, useful for fishing poles and pipes, said one German promoter, and they grew excellent sugar and cotton after they had been cleared. Lighter, well-timbered, *mulatto* soils deposited by the Brazos River were also superior croplands. Farther east, "redlands" embraced more than a hundred-square-mile section between the Sabine and Trinity rivers and grew excellent cotton. Rich black molds under-

6. William Kennedy, *Texas: The Rise, Progress, and Prospects of the Republic of Texas*, p. 63.

7. Ibid., pp. 70–71.

lay the prairies in the west, where the farmer had merely to insert the plowshare, "which encounters no obstacle." A strong oxen team and heavy plow broke through the tight sward, which supplied ample nutrients for corn.[8]

The variety and numbers of interesting and useful wild animals astonished many people and, as we have seen, subsisting on wild game was an incipient way of life on the frontier. An unusual glimpse of this aboriginal abundance comes through the pen of Bishop Marín de Porras, who journeyed through his diocese, which included Texas as far east as Natchitoches, in the spring of 1805. In a letter to the viceroy of New Spain, the Spanish cleric likened the flower-decked countryside east of Goliad to the "pastures of Aranjuez." Beavers filled streams, he reported enthusiastically, and numbers of game animals appeared so high "that it is incredible to one who has not seen them. . . . Even more wonderful to see are the great herds and droves of wild horses and mares that are called mustangs here. As well built as the best of Europe and of an incredible agility . . . they are found close to the roads in herds of four to six thousand head."

Climatically this zone resembled Old Castile, continued de Porras, who admired its natural resources, but not its inhabitants. French-speaking hunters exploited abundant deer for skins and, in winter months, killed innumerable ducks for the New Orleans market. English-speaking squatters lived without law, remarked the cleric, "frightened like wild animals at the sight of their fellow creatures." But nature was truly bountiful in this ill-peopled border zone.[9]

The diversity of potentially useful Texas plants compared favorably with the numbers of animals. Holley, Edward, Muir, Stiff, Kennedy, and others described valuable pines, hardwoods, and aromatic shrubs in the interior rolling zone, which included a large part of the Brazos watershed. Lawrence's *Texas in 1840,* published anonymously, stressed the usefulness of pines, oaks, cypress, elm, and so on for building and fencing in this same region. Live oaks, valuable for shipbuilding, added Kennedy, were more abundant than anywhere else. Spanish moss, although funereal in aspect, made solid, cheap bedding material after being soaked and dried. Pecan trees grew well. The nopal or opuntia cactus, on which the red dye–producing cochineal insect fed, flourished

---

8. Holley, *Texas,* pp. 47, 49, and 52; and Kennedy, *Texas,* pp. 139, 194.

9. Nettie Lee Benson, "Bishop Marín de Porras and Texas," *Southwestern Historical Quarterly* 51 (1947): 26, 27.

in drier, less woody localities in the west. Kennedy described two kinds of cochineal, fine grain and wild, from which six collections could be made annually by scraping off the insects with a blunt knife or rabbit tail. People boiled, dried, and bagged them for export to Mexico. He reported that almost one hundred thousand pounds of cochineal had been shipped from that nation to England in 1831. [10]

Mesquite grass received widespread approval in the Texas "garden" as a year-round fodder on which livestock thrived. Holley noted that "muskit" closely resembled bluegrass and remained alive all winter in a zone between the Guadalupe and Nueces rivers. The grass retained nutritive value even when dry. Others agreed with Holley. Some, like Lawrence, spoke in rather vague terms about rich prairies full of mesquite grass on the Upper Colorado watershed and farther south on other waterways in the west. Kentuckian William McClintock admitted it was equal in pasture or hay to timothy or closed clover back home. Kennedy believed it to be coextensive with the mesquite tree. Olmsted first encountered mesquite grass between Austin and San Marcos. He had heard residents in Central and East Texas describe it in glowing terms and confirmed that his pack animals eagerly fed on it. Horses, sheep, and cattle loved this fine, short grass that made up such excellent pastures across western prairies. [11]

This combination of fine grasses, rich soils, and a virtual year-round growing season made the selection of crops an imaginative and potentially profitable enterprise in Garden Texas. Bollaert repeated a colloquialism about Texas: "If you put ten-penny nails in the ground, you will have a crop of iron bolts." It seemed that all a settler had to do was to scratch a little in the soil (such crude methods offended German Viktor Bracht), drop in seed, and wait for a bumper harvest. Similarly, untended stock thrived, as neither cattle nor poultry reportedly needed attention. In such a place of natural delights and huge returns, little could go wrong, according to authors in the 1830s and 1840s. [12]

In fact, initially, little did appear to go wrong, but as the Brazos River picked up increasing loads of silt from cleared areas and carried them

10. [A. B. Lawrence], *Texas in 1840, or, the Emigrant's Guide to the New Republic*, p. 105; and Kennedy, *Texas*, pp. 92, 97.

11. Holley, *Texas: Observations*, pp. 69–70; [Lawrence], *Texas in 1840*, pp. 108–109; William A. McClintock, "Journal of a Trip through Texas and Northern Mexico in 1846–1848, II," *Southwestern Historical Quarterly* 34 (1930): 150; Kennedy, *Texas*, p. 103; and Frederick Law Olmsted, *Journey through Texas*, pp. 135–36.

12. W. Eugene Hollon and Ruth L. Butler, *William Bollaert's Texas*, p. 287.

off to the bays and estuaries, conditions changed. The image of Garden Texas helped to destroy the very abundance that it was supposed to create. Cotton and sugarcane plantations sprang up along the banks and tributaries of the Brazos River. Colonists slashed down the wild cane, left it to dry, then sent flames shooting tree-high into the edges of woodland, killing surrounding trees as effectively as if by girdling. They waggled hand spikes into softened earth and planted corn, sweet potatoes, and pumpkins. Teams of oxen dragged out tree stumps, tenacious cane roots, and other obstacles. In short, fence rails, logs and planks for houses, and the process and tempo of land clearing loosened the grip of pines, oaks, hickories, and other trees. As their roots died or were dug up, the surrounding soils grew unstable and spring freshets washed them away. But if settlers saw this erosion, they ignored it, for the boosters of the Texas garden promoted land not as home but as commodity. Land was good, cheap, and plentiful. If it gave out, unlimited quantities of it existed farther west. It could be bought and sold for crop after crop of corn and cotton. It took more than a generation of expanding tillage, monocropping, and soil erosion before the image of the capitalist garden lost its bright, ebullient luster.

Lincecum, our "swan watcher," was one of the first Texans to call for restraint. It took a woodsman's eye to spot the problem of ignorance and poor husbandry amid the bustle and boom of burgeoning cropland and yields. In 1861 he wrote about the need to conserve the native pasture grasses that too many cattle and sheep had overgrazed. He lamented the decline in quality of once "boundless unplowed prairies" and condemned the "destructive tramp of immigration." Others saw the tarnished image, too. As early as 1837, Andrew Muir's book talked about "great havoc" among deer. Some settlers shot as many as fifteen hundred annually as a business; and buffalo "are fast disappearing from the plains of the lower country." In less than fifty years, they would be gone forever.[13]

Some old-timers looked back and recognized changes for the worse. One of the "Old Three Hundred," James H. Kuykendall, saw how fine bottomland pastures had vanished and how weeds and scrubby growth invaded fertile places. Overgrazing had taken a toll; so had repeated crops of cotton and corn without any regard for rotation or fertilizer.[14]

13. Lois Wood Burkhalter, *Gideon Lincecum, 1793–1874: A Biography*, pp. 177–78; Andrew F. Muir, ed., *Texas in 1837*, pp. 75, 125; and David B. Edward, *The History of Texas*, p. 74, commented on declines of bison and deer.

14. J. H. Kuykendall, "Reminiscences of Early Texans," p. 52.

Back in the 1830s, however, when members of the Galveston Bay and Texas Land Company were selling East Texas acreage to folk in New England and elsewhere, the image of the garden was pure and unblemished. No provision was required for livestock because "nature's ample store is sufficient throughout the year; and at all seasons they fatten on the natural pastures; of course they multiply rapidly; and Texas may be called the paradise of animals . . . and to man it is the land of promise." Cotton, corn, sugarcane, assorted fruits, and vegetables turned promise into a reality. Early reports confirmed that these new crops prospered together with the army of introduced animals like cattle, hogs, sheep, horses, and mules.[15]

Comparative Advantages

Rhetorical flourishes that made Texas a terrestrial paradise, a veritable "elysium for the florist and painter," required clarification. The physical attributes of the region and its resources were redoubtable, but compared with what? Having used rhetorical devices to capture the public's attention, it was important to make them stick. Promoters solidified the garden image of Texas through comparisons with adjacent states or other regions. These became a benchmark against which the productivity of Texas could be compared and contrasted.[16]

It is instructive to turn again to those writers in the 1830s and 1840s who launched the garden image and who strengthened it by comparisons with other places in North America. Holley made no bones in arguing that Texas was superior to Louisiana, especially with respect to its climate and resources (it is ironic that Holley died in New Orleans from yellow fever). Louisiana, like Texas, had its sea breezes, but miasma from perennial swamps and flood-prone lowlands made human health much more precarious. That is what Holley meant by climatic "blandness" in Texas. The genial influence of southern and northern winds was especially effective, whereas residents "in the low country of the southern United States" did not experience such relief.[17] Selection of prairies for habitation was another element that separated Texas from Louisiana,

15. Galveston Bay and Texas Land Company, *An Address to Emigrants*, p. 6.
16. "Texas," *De Bow's Review* 10 (1851): 627–45.
17. Holley, *Texas*, p. 41; and idem, *Texas: Observations*, p. 121.

where fewer natural openings forced residents to clear land. Natural gases in forest soils inevitably escaped and reportedly brought on fevers.

The almost unqualified praise that Mary Holley gave to Texas was not necessarily borne out in practice, even in the Bolivar area, where she stayed on her visits. Her brother complained five or six months before her first arrival in 1831 that mosquitoes were driving him mad in the summer heat. "They have operated on me at Bolivar like a perpetual blister," said Henry, who was convalescing from a bout with fever. Cousin Stephen took a more detached view and added a certain historical and spatial perspective to Holley's favorable but very colored comparisons.[18]

Stephen F. Austin never doubted that Texas was blessed physically, more so than he had initially hoped. In a letter to a good friend, Joseph H. Hawkins, in July, 1821, he exclaimed that, climatically, the area he had selected for colonization was one of the most delightful "in this, or any other country." Additionally, soils were rich, and the colony's proximity to future seaports promised rewards "which few spots on the globe could furnish to an equal extent."[19]

Several letters from the earlier years attest to the *empresario's* enthusiasm for Texas' climate and agricultural riches. Texas was, Austin claimed, "decidedly superior in point of health and salubrity to any portion of North America in the same parallel." Moreover, bottomlands were less subject to fever and agues than other U.S. river lands below 36° latitude. He noted that conditions were not tropical enough for coffee or cocoa, although coffee did grow successfully in the 1840s, but they enabled cotton, sugar, "and all other productions of Louisiana and Mississippi to succeed very well."[20]

Austin viewed Texas as a geographer would, evaluating its position, tallying up the number of rivers and bays, their navigability, and making a list of the abundance and value of resources and industry. He declared himself well satisfied with what he found. For a country that had lain dormant for so long, his new Texas was making enormous strides. He emphasized that *the country itself had afforded the strongest inducements to emigration by its real and intrinsic value.*"[21] This meant its economic potential, but not exclusively so.

18. Henry Austin to Stephen F. Austin, August 26, 1831 "Austin Papers," 2:690.
19. Stephen F. Austin to [Hawkins], July 20, 1821, "Austin Papers," Vol. 1, pt. 1, p. 402.
20. Stephen F. Austin to David Porter, February 16, 1829, "Austin Papers," 2:166–67.
21. Stephen F. Austin to J. L. Woodbury, July 6, 1829, "Austin Papers," 2:227.

The rolling prairie zone where many of his "family" of settlers lived was his true pleasure. By rambling through that undulating parkland, he experienced "a freedom, a wide and wild and elevated range of thought, as well as action." With an unusual poetic flourish, Austin wrote to his old friend and hunting buddy, Gen. William Ashley, that crowded streets were not for him. In his opinion, urban folk tended to be less resilient on the frontier. He was greatly saddened by the unexpected death of Henry Austin's wife, complaining that as she had come from "brick walls and paved streets," she had not become adjusted to rural living. Like other urban dwellers, the lady's life was too sheltered; it was snuffed out by shocks from rural Texas.[22]

On the other hand, once acclimated, there was a great deal for newcomers to enjoy, especially the freedom of new, open lands. The vitality of being in natural surroundings galvanized them, so that Austin was able to understand the feelings of despair that the Indians must have felt from seeing how settlers cleared out their forests and hunted their game. He admitted, too, that the power of the colonizers, not necessarily their sense of justice, succeeded. Once in motion, the force of what would be called "manifest destiny," the philosophy of acquisition and expansion increasingly practiced by Americans, was irresistible. Or, as Austin put it, "the current of events . . . [could not] be stopped" until the Indians were extinguished or acculturated.[23]

In a way, then, *empresario* Austin anticipated Garden Texas as a space cleared of all human and physical obstacles, a space in which settlers were free to impregnate nature's garden. Enjoyment existed in control and assertion. Cotton and wool were clearly appropriate staples. The first would grow from finest soils in the east, and the second from sheep flocks spread out on the hill grasses in the north, which were "surpassed by none in the country." Compared with his frequent use of the term "wilderness," the metaphor of the garden is scarcely mentioned, but it did have a place, mostly as man-made garden rather than a natural one. It represented the end product of clearing and cultivation so that it was a future garden. Austin's Texas garden, however, demanded people who would be willing to put their shoulders to the wheel and work as one. The image also reflected the need for cooperation and the sense

22. Stephen F. Austin to Gen. William H. Ashley, October 10, 1832, "Austin Papers," 2:871–72; and Austin to Mary Austin Holley, April 20, 1833, "Austin Papers," 2:953.
23. Stephen F. Austin to Gen. William H. Ashley, "Austin Papers," 2:872.

of community and mutual trust, not merely for individual profit and exploitation.[24]

It is, then, scarcely surprising that Holley, who gathered information from Austin, reflected views similar to his about the overall healthfulness and fertility of Texas. She added useful details—for example she recommended October as the best month for immigrants so that newcomers would have several months to adjust before the onset of the hot summer. Biting cold, of course, did occur, as evidenced by the 1830 winter, when severe weather buffeted Texas and killed off Louisiana's orange trees. But an old-timer from Maine told Holley that Texas winters were usually so mild "as not to kill the Lima bean." From what she wrote, Holley believed him.[25]

Kennedy made useful comparisons between Texas and other regions. The young Republic appeared superior to the northeastern United States because it was safe from temperature extremes. It was undoubtedly healthier than Louisiana (for reasons that Holley had offered). Exposure to New Orleans' heat made Kennedy prefer Houston. Houston was poorly situated on a low-lying, moist coastal plain, but the sea breeze cooled it. He was, in fact, able to take "pedestrian exercize with safety in the open prairie at mid-day in the fervid month of June" because the breeze was strong enough to cool him.[26]

This British diplomat used Lawrence's *Guide* to note that January weather in Texas corresponded to May weather in New York City. One man explained that he felt less prostrated by summer heat in Texas than in Princeton, New Jersey, or Philadelphia, Pennsylvania. Kentucky also lagged behind Texas in its soil quality, according to a gentleman's letter to General Combs of Lexington in 1838, which Kennedy also quoted. On the other hand, popularizer Kennedy said nothing to make Texas preferable to lands west of the Rockies.[27]

Detailed comparisons included agricultural products such as cotton, sugarcane, fruits, and, of course, livestock. Again Kennedy was an articulate spokesman, and his comments received widespread attention, especially in Europe. The fact that *Texas* was translated into German suggests how important prospective emigrants believed his opinions to be.

24. Stephen F. Austin to Rhoads Fisher, June 17, 1830, "Austin Papers," 2:427; and Austin to W. H. Wharton, April 24, 1829, "Austin Papers," 2:208.

25. Holley, *Texas: Observations,* p. 123.

26. Kennedy, *Texas,* p. 63; quotation, p. 65.

27. Ibid., p. 68, from [Lawrence], *Texas in 1840,* p. 38; and Kennedy, *Texas,* pp. 78–79.

Kennedy drew from Marryatt's *Diary* about cotton's excellent reputation in Texas and confirmed the latter's claims. Planters achieved a higher yield per acre than in other states because rich soils, genial weather, and a longer growing season, from February to September, assured excellent results, especially in the Colorado, Brazos, Trinity, and Red River valleys. Experts judged cotton to be finer in texture than the best in Louisiana, and better than in Carolina. Merchants in Liverpool, England, admired Texas cotton as well.[28]

Sugarcane was another suitable crop for the Texas garden, where it grew fuller and taller than in Louisiana and had a higher sugar content. The Brazos Valley offered better lands for cane than the Mississippi Valley, argued Kennedy. Others agreed, for although sugarcane was just getting started in Texas, people expected it to thrive there because it was less prone to killing frosts.[29]

Many kinds of fruits grew excellently in Texas, embellishing the land and spelling out profits for horticulture. Except for the apple, for which the coast was too warm, peaches, melons, oranges, figs, plums, bananas, plantains, and spices reportedly flourished. Melons, claimed Lawrence, developed better than "elsewhere known, even Nashville in Tennessee not excepted." Garden produce "might rival the finest exhibition of horticultural success of the older cities of the north," he continued. Even the abundant and widespread native grapes tasted sweeter than similar ones in Arkansas and Louisiana.[30]

The long list of agricultural advantages also singled out livestock. Many authors, including acerbic Olmsted, characterized the western prairie or so-called mountain zone as the best home for cattle and sheep. Fodder and weather conditions were perfect for them. "Texas is, perhaps, one of the finest portions of the world for raising cattle," wrote Orceneth Fisher in his 1841 *Sketches*. Cattle "rolled in luxury" all year on "muskeet" grass. There were no "long dreary" northern winters. Apart from "branding and salting," ranchers could live with little effort as their livestock ranged outdoors all year.[31] Norwegian farmer Elise Waerenskjold gave some "inside" support to that opinion in the 1850s from Van Zandt County, where, she noted, "cattle, horses, and pigs run

28. Kennedy, *Texas,* pp. 84–87; and Woodman, *Guide,* pp. 30, 56, 144.

29. Kennedy, *Texas,* pp. 89, 154; and [Lawrence], *Texas in 1840,* p. 105.

30. Kennedy, *Texas,* p. 94; [Lawrence], *Texas in 1840,* p. 128; and David Woodman, *Guide to Texas Emigrants,* p. 56.

31. Orceneth Fisher, *Sketches of Texas in 1840,* p. 32; and Edward Stiff, *The Texas Imigrant: Being a Narration of the Adventures of the Author in Texas,* p. 134.

about in the woods without any supervision," apparently with few losses from predators.[32]

Kennedy repeated a proverb in this regard: "It will cost more to raise a brood of chickens in Texas than an equal number of cattle." Barnyard fowl required some food and protection from varmints, but stock fended for themselves. In northern states it was well known that "man lives for the beast" by providing hay, "but in Texas the beast lives for man." With a small investment a man could amass a fortune from cattle "by sitting still and letting it grow upon him," proclaimed longtime resident William Dewees, who calculated that a herd would double in size every two years. Innumerable hogs fattened themselves on "mast" from acorns, pecans, and hickory nuts, plus grapes, hackberries, and other wild fruits. Feeding them a little helped make them stay around a farm instead of growing wild: "You can, nine years out of ten, kill your pork out of the woods," declared Dewees.[33]

Agricultural Journals and the Garden

The booster image of Texas as a garden for profit received support in agricultural journals and magazines after about 1840. The first agricultural associations in America were established in 1785 in Pennsylvania and in South Carolina, where innovators experimented with foreign crops, including the olive and grape, and made efforts to improve livestock. In the 1790s similar societies to promote agriculture commenced in New York and Massachusetts; and by the mid-1850s state agricultural societies existed in about twenty states.[34]

Texas, however, was not included among them. Several societies existed on a county level around that time; the most famous was Austin County's Cat Spring, founded in 1856. But progress in the dissemination of agricultural information was comparatively slow, as no state agricultural journal existed until a decade later. Regional magazines acted as the mainstays for information about crops and advice about planting, tending, and harvesting them in Texas. These publications were

32. C. A. Clausen, ed., *The Lady with the Pen*, p. 30.

33. Kennedy, *Texas*, pp. 134–35; and William B. Dewees, *Letters from an Early Settler of Texas*, pp. 301–302.

34. D. J. Brown, "Encouragement of Agriculture in the United States," pp. 15–29, especially pp. 21–22.

strongly progressive in outlook, detailing methods of crop development. They stressed the profit motive rather than the "place-making" value of the land as a home.

One important monthly, the *Southern Cultivator,* published in 1843 out of Athens, Georgia, did much to inform those settlers who wished to leave the Carolinas and "gullies of Georgia" about opportunities in Texas. The journal was the leading farm paper for the lower South in the 1840s and 1850s, and during those two decades it ran seventy-eight articles about Texas. Most of these "letters" appeared after the mid-1850s, when circulation was approximately ten thousand.[35]

De Bow's Review (1846–1880) grew to be another important monthly journal with a definite slant toward southern agriculture. James D. B. De Bow launched his magazine in New Orleans with a ninety-six page issue filled with useful data about crops, commerce, and transportation. After a few years, however, he became so strapped for money that he discontinued publication. A wealthy sugar planter rescued the publication, and after about 1850 subscriptions began to pick up. By the early 1860s, *De Bow's* had achieved the greatest circulation of any southern journal.[36]

At least twenty articles between 1846 and 1860 involved Texas, and many of them included particulars about specific localities, for example, the Rio Grande Valley, Galveston, and Corpus Christi. Almost all of the essays about Texas advocated immigration into this thinly occupied territory, where prospects were excellent. It reportedly surpassed California in agricultural potential, just as California was dominant in minerals. De Bow rejected complaints that Texas was a refuge for ruffians. He solidly defended the state as an agricultural emporium and supplied his readers with a list of its merits.

In 1847, for example, in "Resources and Progress of Texas," De Bow claimed to have assembled accurate data that directed customary superlatives at the soils and climate of Texas. As an agricultural hearth, Texas was expected to play an increasingly important role in the nation's economy. Sugar, cotton, and corn were staples that northern states needed, but tropical fruits, and any crop in Louisiana, also grew well in Texas. In short, "there is no part of the United States where an industrious man can live so easily, and in such abundance, as in Texas." The reader

---

35. Mary Jo Edwards, "Texas Agriculture as Reflected in Letters to the Southern Cultivator Prior to 1861," pp. 2, 5.

36. Frank L. Mott, *A History of American Magazines,* 2:338–48.

was to understand that the "industrious man" could be a Scot, German, Englishman, or native Yankee, but not a "drunkard and an Irishman."[37]

An 1851 issue carried an eighteen-page article entitled "Texas" aimed at those people who were thinking about moving to the state. Louisiana took second place to Texas in this story, whose focus was cotton, but including indigo, tobacco (as good as Cuba's, it was claimed), peaches and yaupon leaves, which brewed into a cheap, acceptable tea. Game animals reportedly were "yet abundant"; and a cornucopia of metals, building stone, and mineral waters presented unheard-of opportunities. The review emphasized the state's beauty, size, location, and fertility.

Emigrants needed to move directly to this "El Dorado of the Southwest," claimed *De Bow's*. But there was literally a fly in the ointment — malicious bugs. Biting insects "will spoil the beauty of the fairest face," complained the author. Therefore, mosquito netting was nearly as important as seeds and farm utensils for the newly arrived immigrant. In all other respects, Texas represented a most pleasing picture, a fertile and profitable garden in the Southwest.[38]

The popular press concentrated on this pragmatic vein. Articles, letters, and notes in newspapers were favorable to emigration, and in the early 1830s the eastern papers took a great interest in prospects for settlement. *The Nashville [Tennessee] Banner* predicted a secure future for stock raising and for the marketing of premium cotton in Texas. The *New York Courier and Enquirer* (November 8, 1834) reported that Texas' population had tripled since 1828, and lands that had once sold for a few cents an acre now fetched five to fifteen dollars. *The [Philadelphia] United States Gazette* applauded emigration; so did the *New York Journal of Commerce* (January, 1835), reporting that Texas cotton commanded a better price than the best from Louisiana.[39]

Many other dailies and weeklies addressed prospects for settlement. The Texas population doubled in the early 1830s, to top fifty thousand by 1836, when independence was declared, and it quadrupled again in the following decade. Newcomers were betting heavily on chances for prosperity. The letters "G.T.T." (Gone to Texas) symbolized escape for some, but pointed to excellent prospects for others — the opportunity

37. "Resources and Progress of Texas," *De Bow's Review* 4 (1847): 318–25, titled *The Commercial Review of the South and West, from 1846–1850*.

38. "Texas," *De Bow's Review* 10 (1851): 627–45.

39. Woodman, *Guide*, pp. 141–76.

metaphorically and literally to break new ground. Some press, of course, was derisive and hostile. A Mobile, Alabama, newspaper called Texas boosterism a hoax. It noted that a steamship was in port with scores of immigrants aboard, some of whom appeared to know all about agues and fevers. "We have heard it said, that even chickens and turkies in that country have touches of the ague" so badly that they shake off their feathers. The paper wished emigrants "God speed."[40]

Government publications took a more dispassionate look at the advantages of Texas. In 1845, the Patent Office authorized a nation-wide agricultural report (more than thirteen hundred pages long) and mailed out circulars to inquire about agricultural productivity.[41] Several Texans replied to the survey. S. W. Kellogg, for example, responded from Robertson County and described conditions between the upper Brazos and Trinity rivers. Wheat grew well in the north, he said; cotton yields were good, but horticulture was just getting under way. Peaches and plums were the only fruits. Kellogg argued that opportunities existed for all types of crops. "The quantity of produce raised in this extent of country may appear small," he remarked, "but six years ago the greatest part of it was used as a hunting ground by the Indians." The implication was obvious: settling a large, but distant Texas was a profitable enterprise.[42]

John Frazer sent back statistics from Jasper County. Cotton dominated the crop picture in terms of market value, with corn and sweet potatoes a distant second and third. Frazer's brief report spoke to the pastoral motif: "The face of the country is gently undulating, and the healthiness of the people is, perhaps, not surpassed by any other country on earth."[43] Forty-one thousand copies of the Patent Office report on crops and livestock were printed in 1848, so that a more sober and sophisticated readership got the chance to peruse the facts and firsthand opinions supplied by Frazer and Kellogg.

Popular journals within Texas should also be mentioned. There was no state agricultural periodical until the late 1860s, but the *Texas Almanac,* founded in 1857, helped to extol the state's garden character in very much a profit-making sense. Carolina-born Willard Richardson, possibly the founder of this annual publication, copied the format

40. Ibid., pp. 157–58.
41. Paul W. Gates, *The Farmer's Age: Agriculture, 1815–1860,* pp. 330–33.
42. S. W. Kellogg to E. Burke, Commissioner, November 14, 1848, in United States, Patent Office, *Report of the Commissioner of Patents for the Year 1848,* pp. 557–61.
43. John Frazer to E. Burke, November 15, 1848, in ibid., pp. 561–62.

of similar compendia in northern states. His basic objective was "to populate Texas." The second volume published accounts of Texas county by county. The contributors to this volume, to which an estimated fifteen thousand to twenty-five thousand people subscribed, wrote "pridefully and a little boastfully but rather honestly," he said.[44]

The *Texas Almanac* was distributed east of the Mississippi River and some copies sold abroad. It "undoubtedly greatly influenced migration to Texas," declared one source, who noted that some people reportedly arrived carrying a family Bible and the *Texas Almanac*. These settlers, and so many others, held on to the idea of a fertile Texas to be exploited. Reports from different sources stressed the many blandishments of the region and compared it favorably with other states.[45]

This idea of Texas as a God-given garden, an Eden capable of sustaining a wide variety of agricultural crops and livestock, can be traced back to European characterizations of North America. Certainly this new land satisfied the image of a pastoral retreat, but more people adopted Zebulon Pike's vision of it in the early 1800s as "one of the richest, most prolific, and best watered countries in North America."[46]

Immigrants' pulses quickened over thoughts of such untapped resources. They talked of boundless expanses of excellent, cheap land. And promoters capitalized on popular images of adjacent states by applying their good qualities to Texas. They also embellished and extended them, making out the Republic to be better than similar regions in the South. Even Olmsted set aside his disdain momentarily by admitting loftily that Texas enjoyed "an Arcadian preeminence of position in the remainder of the nation" and had an "opulent future." This "preeminence" was, of course, quite capable of mismanagement. But in the early 1850s such words fell on deaf ears as a veritable ocean of land beckoned those assertive, courageous individuals willing to make the move to Texas. This image of the garden served to shift opinion away from the view that Texas was a distant and isolated place — a hostile and difficult wilderness — to the vision of a country of unprecedented promise and opportunity.[47]

---

44. Stuart McGregor, "The Texas Almanac, 1857–1873," *Southwestern Historical Quarterly* 50 (1947): 419–30; and the *Texas Almanac for 1858*, pp. 87–88.

45. McGregor, "The Texas Almanac," pp. 427, 429.

46. Kennedy, *Texas*, p. 82.

47. Ibid., p. 82; and Olmsted, *Journey through Texas*, p. 411.

5. The Mediterranean Image in the Southwest

Intrinsic salubrity and fertility that fitted the garden image required a new component, human enterprise, to fully exploit that ideal—agriculturalists would "improve" nature by tapping its resources. The metaphor that described this human activity in the perfect garden revived classical allusions to Mediterranean Europe. People began to imagine fashioning Texas into North America's own Mediterranean, more particularly into its Italy. And the thought was sustained by widespread interest in classical history and culture through the final decades of the 1800s. Settlers would complement the land's physical goodness and natural beauty by building villages with orchards and vineyards and by introducing sheep and goats into those natural pastures filled with flowers. The argument was that, as such landscapes had been the foundation for classical civilization in Greece and Rome, identical efforts with the same plants and animals would bring distinction to Texas. It was both a progressive and a romantic image that appealed to a certain class—those foreign-born, relatively wealthy, and well-educated immigrants.

With a subtropical location and climate and excellent soils, Texas was to be this imaginary hearth in North America, especially for settlers from distant lands who were searching for the ideal pastoral retreat. Woodlands in the east possessed all the advantages and resources of the American South. Drier hills and prairies in the west resembled Old Mexico and its stronghold in the Southwest; they would be important for horticulture and livestock. Together the area that encompassed both east and west contained enormous promise—promoters reminded the public that Western civilization had been born in such a genial, fertile region.

Politicians added rhetoric to this uplifting image. One had simply to consult a world map and follow the parallels of latitude across the Atlantic Ocean into Europe to discover similarities with the Mediterranean and North Africa, including access to a warm sea, in this case, the Gulf of Mexico, across which trade with the torrid zone would be unimpeded. Texas, like Spain, Italy, and Greece, was perfectly situated between tropical and temperate latitudes. It also connected east with west. For twelve years before California completed the geopolitical puzzle of America's "manifest destiny" and eventually preempted the Mediterranean image, Texas stood as the route to the Orient—a path through a romantic wonderland. As a beneficiary of Spanish colonial inheritance, Texas also shared some cultural characteristics with Mediterranean civilization. This cultural affinity was problematic, however; although Hispanic culture in Texas represented a direct link to the actual Mediterranean, white American settlers tended to disparage it. Nonetheless, they adopted the legacy of place names, dress, and aspects of speech and material culture left by Mexican rule. Certainly Stephen F. Austin had no plans for throwing off the Hispanic past. And later Texans, having successfully gained independence and control of the land, would once again celebrate its Mediterranean character.

It is useful to examine the component parts of the image of Texas as a Mediterranean environment and to suggest how individuals drew on the image to promote new agricultural possibilities. That Texas was an intrinsically fertile, unusually bountiful region went unchallenged, even by those detractors who were not especially fond of its inhabitants. It was this natural fecundity that repeatedly drew attention from Austin's time onward. There is, however, an important distinction to be made between this image of a Mediterranean garden and the concept of a Texas "home" in the image of lands left behind in Germany, Scandinavia, England, or even Italy. The Mediterranean motif expressed an outside ideal, not a personal, subjective assessment of the land as a new dwelling place. Except for a very few Italians who did compare Texas and their own country, the "Italian" Texas reflected a highly colored picture of what people wanted Texas to be, not necessarily of what it or the Mediterranean region actually was.

The image of Texas as a Mediterranean—a garden in which peasants tilled fields, grew valuable fruits, and tended numerous herds of cattle,

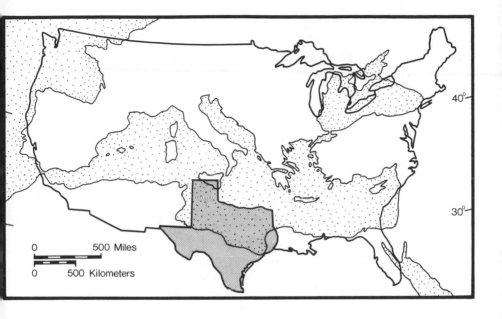

A comparison of U.S. and Mediterranean latitudes, including Texas (after Semple, 1931).

sheep, and goats under azure skies — is especially attractive, as the concept is linked to the origins of Western culture. Art, science, and literature had been nurtured on the Mediterranean shores of present-day Egypt, Greece, Italy, and Spain. The position of this great sea had facilitated contacts between northern Europe, Africa, and Asia. By stressing the historical and cultural importance of Mediterranean Europe, the scene was set for re-creating a similar sense of importance for Mediterranean regions in the New World.

Mediterranean Climate

Texas looked familiar to certain Spanish travelers who likened parts of this isolated, dangerous province of New Spain to "Old Castile." Bishop Marín de Porras drew on this analogy in his fact-finding tour in 1805. Texas lay in the same latitudes as the Old World Mediterranean. A 70° F "isothermal belt" consisting of mean annual temperatures drawn across most of Texas and neighboring Louisiana showed temperatures similar to much of "Spain, Portugal, all of Greece," plus "Syria, Palestine, Persia and the Chinese empire." Similarities in latitude, seasonal temperatures, and moisture regimes inspired writers to discover or invent other analogies.[1]

Commentators claimed that the Texas climate compared favorably with Italy. In general, hot summers and warm winters, with most precipitation occurring in winter and spring, characterize the conventional Mediterranean-type climate. Modern studies classify much of Central and East Texas as possessing a humid mesothermal climate, that is, with normally moist conditions in which plants grow for most of the year under moderate temperatures. Summers are subtropical, with the hottest month averaging above 71.6° F, and precipitation occurs most of the year. The true Old World Mediterranean climate is similar to that of Texas except that the former has more of a summer dry season. Despite Holley's contention that droughty conditions in summer made fevers less prevalent than in the South, East Texas and the Brazos Valley are subject to summer rains. West Texas, however, normally enjoys dry summers, and the moisture deficit reflected by periodic drought makes it a zone for drought-resistant grasses, cacti, and shrubs—a vegetation type common in subtropical steppes and deserts.[2]

Without decades of weather statistics to draw from, William Kennedy and Britisher Ann R. Coleman celebrated Italian elements in the Texas climate. In fact, Kennedy described the whole geographical region as the "Italy of America," blessed with fine temperatures and with "products which render life agreeable." Coleman, an immigrant from English Cumberland, concurred. She especially admired the "Italian sky," in which by night the stars seemed somehow nearer than in Europe. The bright, clear atmosphere in the west made distant planets shine with a remarkable brilliance.

Such thoughts of "Italian" skies most probably did not enter the minds of Mary Rabb or Daniel Shipman, who, as likely as not, had never heard of Italy. But promoters had. Whereas settlers had discovered in very personal ways similarities to landscapes they had left, promoters conjured

---

1. George H. Sweet, *Texas: Her Early History, Climate, Soil and Material Resources,* p. 67.
2. Clyde P. Patton, Charles S. Alexander, and Fritz L. Kramer, *Physical Geography,* pp. 292–300.

up a public image of Texas as Italy that was romantic and certain to please would-be German, British, and other foreign immigrants.[3]

Andrew Muir's *Texas in 1837* picked up the same theme, remarking that "the climate of Texas has been compared with that of Italy." Never having been to Italy, Muir could not base his comparison on experience; however, the clear, warm, and refreshing atmosphere made both days and nights agreeable and fit his idea of what Italy must be like. Flowers, lush grasses, and, of course, wild grapes also made the image plausible. Lawrence chose to improve on the metaphor by saying that Texas certainly had an Italian climate but that its soils were superior. It was a question of time, he stated, before agriculturalists rearranged Texas' appearance to make it as delightful as "are now the scenes where once a Fabius fought, a Tully spoke, and Caesar reigned."[4]

Such windy utterances had a serious purpose. Comparisons with ancient Rome reflected and promoted optimism about both present conditions and future plans for Texas. If the Mediterranean image was an appropriate and persuasive one, then the history of classical civilization could also be transferred to North America's Southwest. Stiff's *Texas Emigrant* put it boldly. "The eagles of Rome, in all her glory, soared not over so fine a country," he declared. Nothing was more favorable to the "development of intellect than Northern Texas." The parallel was simple: by going to Texas, the settler in this new Italy would discover all the essentials for creating a great civilization. Here was the unprecedented opportunity to build a glorious future. "The Spartan mothers never nestled to their bosoms better materials for heroes than will be nursed in Texas," concluded Stiff. His "heroes" were not the ones that most people named, as Stiff had opposed political independence, but such references crop up frequently in colored accounts of the struggle against Mexico. Whether one believed Stiff's lofty thoughts or not did not really matter; what was important was the sense of optimism and enthusiasm that he and others managed to impart by these images. The idea of progress comes through in his well-written account of the trials and difficulties of pioneering in Texas. He advocated settlement in the rolling prairie zone because it represented his ideal country—his

3. William Kennedy, *Texas: The Rise, Progress, and Prospects of the Republic of Texas,* p. 66; and C. Richard King, ed., *Victorian Lady on the Texas Frontier: The Journal of Ann Raney Coleman,* p. 165.

4. Andrew F. Muir, ed., *Texas in 1837,* p. 127; and [A. B. Lawrence], *Texas in 1840, or, The Emigrant's Guide to the New Republic,* p. 126.

"Rome"—free from cruel winters in the north and torrid heat in the south. This was to be the "paradise of the world."[5]

Holley, a trend maker in her characterizations of Texas, made no explicit mention of the Italian motif, but on one occasion in 1838, she imagined that a prairie fire across the San Bernard River was "an irruption of Vesuvius. It is sublime." Her desire to be a writer of romantic literature doubtless accounts for this epithet in her journal. Perhaps she did not conjure up the Mediterranean image as distinctly as others did because she relied heavily on her mentor, Stephen F. Austin, who tended to describe the country in a more restrained and factual manner.[6]

Austin's description of Texas, which he intended for Europeans to read after the 1830 law closed the region to United States immigrants (although he obtained an exemption for his colony), made no direct comparison of places with which foreign settlers could identify. However, an earlier pamphlet that the Galveston press published mentioned growing vines, olives, and similar fruit from "a temperate Southern latitude." Mexican official Juan Almonte was more specific. The true temperate lands were in the Department of Béxar, particularly around San Antonio, where "grapes, olives and all other products common to the temperate zone" supposedly flourished. He noted that folk from the western edge of the Mediterranean Sea, Canary Islanders, numbering fifty-seven, were making excellent progress in that city.[7]

Although images of a new Italy in Texas appealed to foreigners, reality proved somewhat different. Caroline von Hineuber, daughter of the first German settler in Texas, Friedrich Ernst, mentioned that after coming to Texas in 1831, her father wrote to friends back home that Texas was a veritable wonderland. It had a republican government, fertile soils, and a climate similar to Italy's. Early years in Texas, however, failed to solidify that image for young Caroline. She had to unfurl an umbrella over her bed in the cabin when it rained. Cattle munched the moss that the family used to cover the sides of the home, and the clay and log chimney looked so dangerous that the Ernsts did not dare light a fire. Her father grew tobacco and sold cigars in San Felipe while they occupied this "doorless and windowless six-cornered pavilion about three

5. Edward Stiff, *The Texas Emigrant: Being a Narration of the Adventures of the Author in Texas*, pp. 135 (first quotation), 136 (second quotation), 202 (third quotation).

6. Mary Austin Holley, *Mary Austin Holley: The Texas Diary, 1835–1838*, p. 51.

7. Eugene C. Barker, "Description of Texas by Stephen F. Austin," *Southwestern Historical Quarterly* 28 (1924): 98–121, especially pp. 99–100; and Juan Almonte, "Statistical Report on Texas," *Southwestern Historical Quarterly* 28 (1925): 187–88.

years." Friedrich Ernst's letter, however, aroused a great amount of interest. Caroline reported that it triggered a whole migration of Germans to Texas.[8]

In a similar but less exaggerated vein, Edward Smith, who penned a detailed account of his journey to Texas in 1849 to make a survey for an English colony, made explicit reference to Italy. He was most impressed by the agricultural potential of the upper Brazos River Valley with its Italian climate. The London-based Texas Emigrant and Land Company to which Smith was attached published a prospectus for emigrants. Climatically, it said, Texas realized "all that poets have sung of the Aegean," and described it as the "Italy of America." Middle-class British emigrants were doubtless stirred by thoughts of sun, blue skies, and warm, clear air.[9]

Authors stressed this image of Texas as Italy from the mid-1830s until at least the mid-1870s. They found it a useful and very positive analogy. Few writers and even fewer settlers had any firsthand knowledge of what Italy actually looked like. They envisaged the picturesque and pastoral countryside that landscape artists painted and gentlemen making "the tour" described. It extended the idea of Garden Texas.

But there was a more practical aspect to that image. It involved the arrival of health seekers and recreationists who visited Texas after railroads made the state more accessible. Many consumptives came "to take the cure" in the dry, sunlit uplands of the American Southwest, and San Antonio was the gateway to this region in Texas. There, an atmosphere, seasons, and verdure like southern Europe served as a backdrop for the color and traditions of the Hispanic culture, reflected by the historic "City of Missions." The physical verisimilitude, culture history, and Spanish traits combined to make Texas North America's Mediterranean in a more real and complete sense.

In *Health-Seekers,* Billy Jones noted that when the Southern Pacific Railroad's Sunset Route arrived in San Antonio in 1877, a veritable army of health seekers descended on the city. In that decade at least a dozen towns within a hundred-mile radius rose to prominence. Uvalde, Boerne,

---

8. Caroline von Hineuber, "Life of German Pioneers in Early Texas," *Quarterly of the Texas State Historical Association* 2 (1899): 227–32; and Rudolph L. Biesele, *The History of German Settlements in Texas, 1831–1861,* pp. 43–44, mentions that Ernst's published letter referred to the climate as being like southern Italy.

9. Edward Smith, "Account of a Journey through Northeastern Texas," *East Texas Historical Journal* 7 (1969): 78–109; 8 (1970): 29–91; and Texas Emigration and Land Company, *Emigration to Texas,* pp. 6, 16.

Luling, and others became resorts whose mineral waters soothed invalids and dyspeptics journeying in from San Antonio. Later, access to California via the Sunset Route enabled travelers to "see the American Italy and live" rather than "see Rome and die!" Why go to Europe was the question, when there was a "combination of Italy, Spain and Switzerland" on the West Coast? Getting there, however, was trying and involved journeying beyond the more accessible Texas through the "American Sahara" in Arizona and Southern California. This post–Civil War boom of the health frontier in California was important for Texas, as the state was almost as popular among migrant invalids as were California and Colorado.[10]

Initially, residents in the Southwest welcomed people with pulmonary afflictions, that is, until 1882, when Robert Koch isolated the tubercle bacillus, proving tuberculosis to be contagious. Newcomers sought out the rarefied, dry, warm, West Texas air as a tonic for health. Some medical practitioners sent patients to winter on the coast because the marine littoral, it was supposed, had smaller temperature changes due to the warming subtropical winds off the Gulf. Visitors in West Texas, parts of which were supposedly as dry as the desert flanking the River Nile, could hunt, camp, and take plenty of exercise daily. Getting back to nature on the coast was more genteel in winter (and more mosquito-free). Duck hunters found it a paradise, but shell collectors, painters, and beach walkers enjoyed it as well.[11]

San Antonio, positioned between the desert and the sea, represented the "Golden Mean"—away from extremes of climate and relief—just as Texas represented a similar classical-like Golden Mean for the entire nation. Muir's book reported that the fresh-looking city outskirts were "covered with works of art, that reminds one of Washington Irving's description of the green valleys of Granada." Later, the church ruins inside San Antonio reminded him of Italy. Visitors who came to the city for their health discovered and commented on similarly unusual and attractive characteristics.[12]

10. Billy M. Jones, *Health-Seekers in the Southwest, 1817–1900*, pp. 71, 87, 103 (quotation); idem, "A Burden on the Southwest: Migrant Tuberculars in the Nineteenth Century," *Southwestern Social Science Quarterly* 47 (1966): 59–67; and John W. Hanson, *The American Italy: Southern California*, pp. 16, 33, 37.

11. Jones, "A Burden," p. 59; and M. K. Taylor, "The Climate of Southwestern Texas and Its Advantages as a Winter Health Resort," *Transactions of the American (Clinical and) Climatological Association* 5 (1888): 209–22, especially p. 212.

12. Muir, *Texas in 1837*, pp. 94 (first quotation), 98 (second quotation).

Guides for the Southern Pacific's Sunset Route focused on Mediterranean aspects of life in San Antonio. It was, according to Galveston, Harrisburg, and San Antonio Railway Company brochures, a sophisticated health resort with spas, sulfur springs, flower-decked walks, quaint streets, and shaded river banks. It was also unique; "a Spanish town today, and the only one where any considerable remnant of Spanish life exists in the United States," was the claim. The idler could watch Indian women dress subtropical "leopard" and ocelot skins with the animals' brains to keep them supple. Mexican women sold caged mockingbirds and cardinals. Then, of course, there was the Alamo, "the monument of a battle greater than Thermopylae; for while one Greek lived to tell the story of heroic defense, not one Texan ever opened his lips to tell how his fellows died."[13]

Such allusions to the classics survived to the turn-of-the-century, but they made the point that this borderlands region had a unique stamp that combined the Old Mediterranean past—San Antonio born of Spanish ambition to stop France's spread westward represented a "religio-martial" existence—with a Southern present. This cosmopolitan mixture of cultures inspired Gov. Oran M. Roberts to an even more grandiose and exotic analogy in claiming San Antonio to be the "Baghdad of America."[14]

The most pretentious use of historical and classical allusions, however, comes from H. F. McDanield and N. A. Taylor, who in 1877 published an account of their adventures in *The Coming Empire; or, Two Thousand Miles in Texas on Horseback*. Texas was truly a "grand tour" for these gentlemen in the traditional European sense of passing several months in offbeat places, usually in southern climes. On such visits it was customary to adopt a condescending stance; one made disparaging remarks about residents while appreciating the allegorical significance of the scenery.

San Antonio looked like Constantinople to the two men. The adjacent Hill Country was Greece, although the travelers admitted they had never been there. Sisterdale's skies and climate and Kerrville's approaches had classical touches. "Kerrville is really named Athens!" they exclaimed. Its residences, churches, and schools looked so beautiful—the scene was

13. Galveston, Harrisburg, and San Antonio Railway Company, *Western Texas as a Winter Resort*, pp. 3, 11–12; and idem, *Immigrants Guide to Western Texas: Sunset Route*, p. 23.

14. Herbert Durand, *The City of Missions, San Antonio, Texas*, p. 3; and O. M. Roberts, *A Description of Texas*, p. 20.

perfect; it lacked only the Parthenon. Farther west, the Pecos River became the River Nile but had a more enduring flow. "The Nile has enriched a nation, that gave letters and civilization to the world; and my Pecos has enriched a nation that has yet to be," was the conclusion.[15]

McDanield and Taylor were not the first visitors to allude to the Nile in West Texas. Teresa Vielé, an officer's wife in Ringgold Barracks, caught her first glimpse of the Rio Grande and thought immediately of Egypt and the River Nile. "It only wanted a few swarthy, turbaned men, and a sphynx or two, to complete the illusion," she wrote. She soon tired of the dreary land, however, declaring that "it seems to hate civilization." But other people had great hopes for the Rio Grande Valley. One report in *De Bow's,* anticipating the valley's sugarcane production by more than a hundred years, judged that cane would do well upstream as far as Laredo. Irrigation was the key. With such a system, El Paso's tradition of horticulture and vines could be reproduced on the Rio Grande's lower reaches.[16]

By 1900, talk of classical antiquity and of sublime or picturesque scenery in West Texas and its gateway, San Antonio, had diminished, partly because these cultural conventions were changing nation-wide and partly because such allusions grew tiresome with experience. People became more curious about odd and unusual things, the novelties of Texas, rather than about the Old World imagery promoted in earlier years. There was reportedly more to do in San Antonio than in similar California towns because San Antonio and its hinterland had "bizarre" qualities suitable for the "Kodak-snapper." But a Missouri Pacific brochure was quick to assure readers that the city had seventy-five miles of sewers and a five-dollar fine for expectorating in public. It was appropriately antiseptic. No fogs existed, as in California and Florida, and winters were milder than in New Mexico and Colorado, so that this tourist center was truly the health seekers' earthly paradise.

After a bath in warm, sulfur-laden water, the visitor could embark on a photo tour of the Mexican quarter's quaint *jacales,* with their exotic filth and assortment of hairless dogs, sombreros, and "lazy" husbands. The city remained a "fair representation of Spain, Egypt, Mexico and

15. H. F. McDanield and N. A. Taylor, *The Coming Empire; or, Two Thousand Miles in Texas on Horseback,* pp. 152 (first quotation), 328 (second quotation).

16. Teresa Vielé, *Following the Drum: A Glimpse of Frontier Life,* pp. 99 (first quotation), 151 (second quotation); and "The Valley of the Rio Grande," *De Bow's Review* 2 (1846): 363.

America. It is at once a Cairo, a Mexico, and a miniature St. Louis."
It was full of missions, battlefields, flowers, bird songs, and curiosities.
Some Mediterranean aspects of San Antonio's physical surroundings,
history, and traditions continued to attract attention. Brochures drew
attention to the many small parks that reflected human values rather
than grandiose allusions. They pointed out the Spanish love for foun-
tains, rare foliage, and flowers. In sum, the city combined "modern util-
ity and beauty with the romance and heroism of the medieval."[17]

But not all analogies between Texas and the Mediterranean were the
product of mere boosterism. Just before Thanksgiving, 1901, Italian
sculptor Pompeo Coppini left his adopted home in New Jersey for San
Antonio. He journeyed by train for four days and finally emerged in
"real Italian sunshine, with the same gorgeous blue sky." Tropical plants
in parks, blooming flowers, and the intimate, neighborly quality of old
houses and streets reminded him of Sicily. Relaxed, friendly ways and
sincere hospitality made Coppini think that the "real America" existed
in Texas. An Italian artist had found his home away from home. Yet
it was not an Italy, capable of attracting large numbers of Italians, for
in the main, the Mediterranean image was a distinctly American one,
designed to appeal to the romantic notions of Englishmen, Germans,
and other north Europeans.[18]

Mediterranean Crops

Mention of fruits, flowers, and vines occurs very often in nineteenth
century books and articles about Texas. Apples did not prosper in hot,
humid conditions, but peaches, oranges, nectarines, figs, and other plants
that we commonly associate with southern Europe did. The Carolinas,
Georgia, Florida, and, later, California, enjoyed reputations for excellent horticulture. Texas was well represented by similar subtropical fruits.
Austin, Holley, and other people took an early, keen, and active interest
in planting orchards and in making house plots and gardens bloom with
fruit, vegetables, and ornamental flowers. Early experiments with horti-

17. Missouri Pacific Railway Company, *San Antonio as a Health and Pleasure Resort,*
pp. 23 (first and fourth quotations), 27 (second quotation), 28 (third quotation); and
Missouri, Kansas, and Texas Railway Company, *Sunny San Antonio,* p. 7.
18. Pompeo Coppini, *From Dawn to Sunset,* pp. 71–72.

culture made the aesthetic and economic details of Mediterranean imagery seem more real and more tangible.

These efforts also made Texas stand out from neighboring states. U. P. Hedrick, who studied early American horticulture, judged that the region within the Louisiana Purchase of 1803 had ample possibilities for the development of horticulture, but residents neglected to reproduce horticultural situations that existed in the Carolinas and Georgia. Few notable orchards and vegetable plots appeared in Louisiana, and the first large orchards in Mississippi, near Vicksburg, date from about 1850. Similar orchards and nurseries appeared in Arkansas a decade later, but by that time, several notable fruit growers, such as Gilbert Onderdonk and Thomas Affleck, had sparked a lively interest in horticulture in Texas. These innovators developed new varieties of fruits and vegetables, planting orchards to test varieties of peaches, plums, and citrus, and contributing solidly to the image of Texas as the American Mediterranean.[19]

Half a dozen or so plants and animals come readily to mind when we think of rural landscapes in the Mediterranean. We have images of vineyards, orchards filled with peaches or figs, olive groves set beside hamlets and villages. Flocks of sheep and goats tended by shepherds browse on surrounding hillsides. People emphasized some of these features in the early stages of Texas settlement. Native vines, for example, grew abundantly, festooning trees along creeks and waterways in the rolling prairie zone. Authors glowingly referred to the need to establish viticulture and to make Texas equal to anything in southern France, Spain, or Italy.

A good deal of argument exists about grape nomenclature, especially that used by travelers and settlers. The mustang grape (*Vitis candicans*) is widespread in Texas, growing best in wooded areas along waterways. The post-oak grape (*V. lincecomii*) is more restricted to central and east counties, where there are sandy soils with oaks and pines. The summer or pigeon grape (*V. aestivalis*), a roadside-dwelling plant, is found usually in sandy thickets and woods. Two other species exist, the muscadine or scuppernong (*V. rotundifolia*) and fox grape (*V. vulpina*), both of which grow mainly in East Texas in moist bottomlands and in shaded places.[20]

19. U. P. Hedrick, *A History of Horticulture in America to 1860*, pp. 351–58.
20. Robert A. Vines, *Trees, Shrubs, and Woody Vines of the Southwest*, pp. 713, 723, 727, 731.

Two factors were important to the spread of grape cultivation in Texas. First, a number of travelers saw for themselves or heard about a tradition of wine making in the Rio Grande Valley around El Paso. Second, they noted the widespread distribution and abundance of native grapes. The most famous was the large mustang species, whose thick serpentine stem reached high into tree canopies. Accordingly, writers concluded that wine making had excellent prospects in Texas and eagerly reported that palatable beverages made from native grapes could be produced in such places as New Braunfels. Therefore, the use of grapes dating back to the eighteenth century in the border region, and the variety and plenitude of native species, convinced authors that Texas would surely become as prominent in viticulture as were Spain or Italy.

These judgments were partly correct. Bartlett, who experienced that "living tornado" of mustangs on his boundary survey in Texas, drank "mediocre" wine from El Paso's vineyards in the early 1850s. Grapes, pears, quinces, onions, and pumpkins grew extensively in the upper Rio Grande Valley. They came originally from the Old World Mediterranean, from Spanish or mission stock. Cultivators trimmed the grape vines back each year, covered them with straw to protect them from the cold, and then irrigated them in spring. Ripe grapes supplied the table from July, and some were turned into raisins and brandy. Men placed ripened grapes in rawhide bags, trod on them, and after two or three weeks, allowed the fermented crude wine to drip into barrels, which were then sold in northern Mexico. Kennedy had heard about these wines and quoted von Humboldt's opinion that they were good enough eventually to make the uplands of Mexico and Central America equal to France, Italy, and Spain in supplying the entire American continent.[21]

Other people were much less enthusiastic. One observer examined the El Paso industry in the late 1850s and thought it primitive and in need of improvements. He estimated production at about 250 to 300 gallons per acre, but dropping; however, with "American skill" he hoped that the volume would soon be doubled to make the El Paso area "the Eden for the grape in the United States." With due care and attention, the upper Rio Grande Valley would be unrivaled even by California, where similar mission grapes existed. A new vineyard of El Paso grapes near San Antonio was also expected to prosper.[22]

21. John Russell Bartlett, *Personal Narrative of Explorations and Incidents in Texas, New Mexico, California, Sonora and Chihuahua*, 1: 185–86; and Kennedy, *Texas*, p. 91.
22. H. C. Williams, "Native Grapes of Arkansas and Texas," in U.S. Patent Office, *Report of the Commissioner of Patents for the Year 1859: Agriculture*, pp. 30–41.

In addition, new Texans had extracted a "pleasant" wine from indigenous grapes, according to Kennedy, and he expected German settlers from "Rhenish provinces" to become vintners. Kennedy's expectations were never met to the degree he had envisioned, but people did report some wines fermented from native grapes. Hermann Seele, for example, enjoyed mustang wine and grape preserves in pastor Louis Ervenberg's home in New Braunfels on Christmas Eve, 1849. Polish peasants from Upper Silesia tried the native muscadine grapes, which Americans said were excellent for wines, but the fruit was too sour for most of them.[23]

The *Almanac* in 1868 had heady words for wine lovers. It declared that "all of northern and central Texas is capable of becoming one vast vineyard." Samuel B. Buckley, who became state geologist, was more precise. He looked back across the ocean and saw in his mind's eye how islands and places with limestone plateaus and volcanic soils wafted by sea breezes like those in Italy and Greece produced noteworthy wines. The long coast of Texas was visited by similar sea breezes, and vines flourished on well-watered limestone hills under a genial sun. Although there were no recent volcanic soils, the granites around Burnet and Llano weathered nicely. Except for perhaps California, concluded Buckley, "Texas has advantages for grape culture over any one of the United States," especially where lands sold for fifty cents to five dollars an acre.[24]

It remained for Thomas Volney Munson (1843–1913) to put Texas on the map in regard to grape cultivation and research. As a student, Illinois-born Munson grew interested in Texas pomology. In 1876, he moved to Denison, Texas, and found the rough limestone country along the banks of the Red River in Grayson County full of wild grapes. He committed his life to viticulture and attracted international acclaim with his research. His important classification of native species rested in large part on specimens he collected in Texas. The botanical research that he conducted as a special agent with the U.S. Department of Agriculture included the development of grape hybrids, control of diseases, and procedures for cultivation and improvement. Munson assembled a unique

23. Hermann Seele, *The Cypress and Other Writings of a German Pioneer in Texas,* p. 97; Frederick Law Olmsted, *A Journey through Texas,* p. 170; see also "Texas Items," *Southern Cultivator* 16 (1858): 369; and T. Lindsay Baker, *The First Polish Americans: Silesian Settlements in Texas,* p. 51.

24. Samuel B. Buckley, "Grapes and Grape Culture in Texas," *Texas Almanac for 1868,* pp. 23, 69.

collection of grape specimens from around the world. In 1888, the French government awarded him the Legion of Merit for his invaluable guidance in saving France's vineyards from the devastating root blight of *Phylloxera*. The pomologist reportedly grafted European grapes onto Texas mustang roots, which are naturally resistant to this New World disease. In this way, the Texas Mediterranean came to the rescue of its French counterpart.[25]

For several reasons, olives and dates never prospered in Texas, and California became their home. But figs, peaches, oranges, and similar fruits that we generally associate with southern Europe did do well, and many books and periodicals mentioned them. Settlers in the Austin Colony, including the *empresario* himself, took an active interest in oranges and peaches.

Austin's house plan reserved space for an orchard, and orange trees were to be set in the front yard. In 1832, Austin notified his brother-in-law, James Perry, about peach, fig, and orange trees awaiting him in Brazoria. Austin's cousin Henry had grapes and plums available, too. About a year later, Austin contacted his sister, Emily, Perry's wife, about two hundred to three hundred peach trees being delivered by wagon; he was most concerned about getting them planted. In one of his last letters, on December 15, 1836, again to Perry, Austin showed his interest in plants for landscaping. He always advised that shade trees and pecans should never be felled near a dwelling. On this occasion, he mentioned that the "seed of the *Ratama* tree should be carefully planted about the first of February," a month he did not live to enjoy.[26]

Mary Holley continued the family's interest in garden plants and horticulture. She claimed to have introduced the strawberry plant to Texas in 1831, and lavished attention on vegetables and flowers, especially roses, during her several visits to Texas. "I love to work in the open air," she wrote. "I took a hoe and employed a boy and myself, clearing away rubbish about the yard and garden." Holley admonished settlers to bring seeds and fruits of all kinds, as did Elise Waerenskjold thirty years later. Conditions were perfect, Holley continued, for warm, tem-

25. Thomas V. Munson, *Foundations of American Grape Culture*, pp. 6–8, 230.

26. Austin to Perry, February 10, 1832, "Austin Papers," 2:748; Austin to Emily Perry, about January 1833, "Austin Papers," 2:921; Austin's house plan, "Austin Papers," 2:719; and Austin to Perry, about December 15, 1836, *Austin Papers*, 3:477.

perate, and tropical produce, and by the mid-1830s, oranges, figs, and peaches were available "in great profusion." People even expected the date palm to grow.[27]

Holley's enthusiasm for horticulture found ample backing from other authors in the 1830s and 1840s. Book sections about growing plants emphasized the variety of fruits and vegetables possible in large part to Texas' southerly latitude and enormous size. Lawrence's *Texas in 1840*, for example, placed figs, oranges, and peaches in coastal areas; apples, pears, and plums grew inland and farther north. Similarly, Ikin's *Texas*, written about the same time, noted that people commonly cultivated figs and peaches; almonds, pawpaws, cherries, and nectarines prospered equally well. This smorgasbord of horticultural products, even though it was bolstered by exaggeration and wishful thinking, remained impressive.[28]

Other popular sources left readers in no doubt about Mediterranean-based horticulture. The *Texas Almanac* affirmed that "Texas is destined to be one of the finest fruit producing countries on this continent." Dr. Ashbel Smith joined the chorus of acclaim when *De Bow's* carried his suggestion that a state agricultural society be established to share knowledge and encourage experimentation. The same agriculturally oriented periodical carried a projection about cropland acreages, speculating that a population in excess of 200,000 (in 1850) could easily be multiplied 250 times and still not exhaust resources. *De Bow's* published statistics suggesting that Texas equaled Louisiana in cropland, exceeded Arkansas, easily beat Florida, and was chasing totals in South Carolina and Mississippi; yields were good and prospects were even better.[29]

If one followed U.S. Patent Office agriculture reports, as many journal editors did, it was clear that Texas had a great future in both traditional cash crops and horticulture. The mid-1850s were very active years for introducing and experimenting with new crops in the United States. Officials supplied seeds and cuttings. Wheat from Mediterranean lands,

27. Holly, *Mary Austin Holley*, p. 67; idem, *Texas*, pp. 65–66; and Samuel W. Geiser, *Horticulture and Horticulturists in Early Texas*, p. 4.

28. [Lawrence], *Texas in 1840*, pp. 145–47; Arthur Ikin, *Texas: Its History, Topography, Agriculture, Commerce, and General Statistics*, pp. 47–48.

29. *Texas Almanac for 1868*, p. 8; "Public Lands of Texas," *De Bow's Review* 13 (1852): 53–56; Ashbel Smith, "Agriculture in Texas," *De Bow's Review* 18 (1855): 200–201; and "Miscellany," *De Bow's Review* 32 (1866): 211.

wild grapes from Arkansas and Texas, and fruits and vegetables from the Orient flooded the U.S. Patent Office, which then funneled these items to growers across the nation. Acorns from Spanish cork oak, tea plants, grape slips, pyrethrum, and camphor were all tested as fiscal cutbacks forced curtailments in the dissemination of more common garden and field plants.[30]

Efforts at crop acclimatization included Texas, where tea appeared to be promising. An 1857 map suggested that all of the state except the coastal region was well adapted for tea plantations. Three published statements from cultivators in Caldwell, Brazoria, and Houston counties made favorable remarks about its value as livestock feed: introduction was a "matter of deep importance, meriting richly the earnest attention of cultivators of the soil, especially of upland districts," concluded I. H. S. Stanley of Houston.[31]

State geologist Buckley's *Preliminary Report of the Geological and Agricultural Survey of Texas* in 1866 summarized the agricultural situation. Texas excelled in grains and cotton; orchard products had almost quadrupled in value during the decade. His list of fruits was a long one and included berries, persimmons, and vines, so that in place of "bringing canned fruit from the New York market, we should have a surplus to send there." He noted that fruit culture would soon become a leading business for many people, and sizable profits were obtainable from a few acres without the costs associated with cotton, grains, sugarcane, and tobacco. An advantageous growing season, weather, soils, and, of course, location in southern North America made all this possible.[32]

The Golden Mean

The *Texas Almanac* (1876) drew a parallel between Texas and "the Byzantium Kingdom of old." Like ancient Constantinople, Austin or San Antonio, some said, and certainly Texas in general, were on the "cross-

30. Charles Mason, "Report of the Commissioner of Patents," in U.S. Patent Office, *Report of the Commissioner of Patents for the Year 1856*, pp. v–vi.

31. United States, Patent Office, *Report of the Commissioner, 1857*, plate IV; and idem, "Sorghum Canes," p. 223.

32. Samuel B. Buckley, *A Preliminary Report of the Geological and Agricultural Survey of Texas*, pp. 61–62, 68.

roads of the commercial highways of the earth." The state stood between the U.S. hinterland in the north and Mexico's mineral treasure in the south. This stress on locational advantage occurred repeatedly, and it echoed the classical idea of a "Golden Mean." If Greece possessed optimal physical conditions, so did Texas, the "Eureka of America," as *De Bow's* stated; and as Greece was in its day the center of the known or inhabited world, so was Texas.[33]

Matthew Fontaine Maury (1806–1873), geographer and naval officer, drew public attention to "our Mediterranean," the Gulf of Mexico. This perfectly located sea, midway between Europe and Asia, had a total drainage basin of about 4.3 million square miles—from the Amazon and Orinoco rivers in the south to the upper reaches of the Mississippi River in the north. The general north-to-south flow of rivers across rather than along parallels of latitude ensured that goods from physically distinct regions could be distributed easily and directly by maritime commerce. Nature had seen fit to make the Gulf of Mexico and its hinterland much larger than the Mediterranean Sea and its drainage basin, noted Maury. Texas and Florida rivers occupied over half a million square miles of watershed, more than the River Nile. Such river basins were far more important than the Nile basin because the temperate (not torrid) latitudes through which the rivers flowed were the homeland for man "in the true nobleness of his being," where he is "neither pinched with hunger, nor starved with cold, as in the frigid [zone], nor surfeited to plethora, as in the torrid zone." In that sense, Texas was far superior to the Nile watershed, which drained only the equatorial or torrid zone of Africa.[34]

In sum, "the exceeding great resources of our Mediterranean beggar description," declared Maury. A perpetual summer along Gulf shores meant that ports could continuously handle traffic in "the fruits of every clime, the staples of every country." The Gulf could become, therefore, "the center of the world" and the focus of international commerce, particularly after the connection with the Pacific Ocean across the Isthmus of Panama was finished. Maury was also interested in a transcontinental rail-sea link to China via Memphis, Tennessee, and Monterrey, Mexico,

33. George A. Ferris, "Stock Raising in Texas," *Texas Rural Almanac*, p. 99; and "Texas," *De Bow's Review* 14 (1853): 68.
34. Matthew F. Maury, "Great Commercial Advantages of the Gulf of Mexico," *De Bow's Review* 7 (1849): 510–23.

passing through Texas. He had no doubt that water traffic through the Mississippi system into the Gulf heralded a new order. Civilization was destined to flourish and progress in the United States. A God-given design based on biblical revelation informed all of science and gave purpose to American expansion.[35]

Some of this optimistic thinking carried over to Texas ports in which others discovered a marine setting and daily bustle like southern Europe's. Indeed, many of the early commercial fishermen who set their seine nets in the bays and estuaries around Galveston, Indianola, and Rockport in the 1870s and 1880s were of Greek and Italian extraction. One federal fisheries expert described the busy dawn scene around the wharf in Galveston. The "mosquito fleet" of perhaps one hundred small sailboats bobbed in the harbor as local men sold their catches of fish, turtles, and farm goods, which they had ferried from various small communities, to wholesalers who supplied restaurants and food stores. He said, "One may find here a load of oysters, there potatoes, in another boat cauliflower and pigs, chickens here and terrapins there, ducks and crabs, fish and milk." One can almost hear the cacophony of grunting stock, squawking fowl, and the animated voices and exclamations of dealers who spoke in Spanish, Italian, or Greek dialects against a backdrop of surging waves and slapping rigging.[36]

Galveston assumed, for some travelers, a certain charm by the 1870s and 1880s. It was a city in the sand, but orange and myrtle trees, as well as roses and oleanders, for which it became famous, anchored the shifting substrate and added a tropical atmosphere. "In the morning the air is heavy with the perfumes of blossoms; in the evening the light, to Northern eyes, is intense and enchanting," explained a visitor. "The approach from the mainland will instinctively remind the traveller of Venice," he noted, so that although problems from mosquitoes and questions about health remained, the visual aspects of the sea-girt city and its Mediterranean symbolism improved.

Another comment captured the texture of the city in moonlight, when the luminescence of buildings and sandy streets produced a "weird and mystic influence in the scene." So strong was the image of Venice that

35. Ibid., p. 523 (first and third quotations), p. 517 (second quotation); and idem, *Physical Geography of the Sea*, pp. xiii, 335.

36. Charles H. Stevenson, "Report on the Coast Fisheries of Texas," in U.S. Commission of Fish and Fisheries, *Report of the Commissioner for 1889 to 1891*, p. 403.

an observer looked in vain for "towers, domes, and minarets, glittering" in the final rays of the evening sun, but was nonetheless pleased by the cosmopolitan spirit of Galveston's inhabitants.[37]

Farther south, a newspaper column from the same period talked about Corpus Christi as the "Gibraltar of the Gulf," uniquely positioned as a disembarkation point for trails to California and Mexico. West of Galveston was Houston, where one could walk "beneath skies that seemed Italian," and where the aroma from roses and magnolias saturated the air. The voyage from Galveston up Buffalo Bayou to Houston's dockside was a pleasure in itself to some. One visitor on the final stage by steamer remarked, "Twilight had passed into night. The passengers and a portion of the crew had gone to rest. The whole river offered a wondrous scene. The bayou seemed converted into a subterranean stream, though much more lovely than the gloomy waters of Greek mythology. I, too, was soon lulled to sleep by the motion of the vessel."[38]

Not everyone was pleased. Some of the early vessels caught fire or sank after their boilers exploded. More fortunate passengers enjoyed watching or taking shots at alligators. At night, ship braziers cast eerie shadows on bankside vegetation as vessels zigzagged up the narrow waterway. Arrival on the Texas mainland in these conditions added awe and wonder.

Admirably located in a "happy latitude," Texas seemed to offer the best of all possible worlds. Its three physical divisions provided three distinct agricultural opportunities. The "peach lands" in the coastal zone grew superior sugarcane, and better-drained "elm" soils produced abundant cotton. Timber, tobacco, rice and "inter-tropical" crops in the Gulf states also did well, so that there was no need to seek them in foreign regions like the Amazon basin, where heat and moisture were so oppressive.[39]

---

37. Edward King, *The Great South*, p. 101 (first quotation), p. 102 (second quotation); and Alexander E. Sweet and J. Amory Knox, *On a Mexican Mustang, through Texas, from the Gulf to the Rio Grande*, pp. 21–22 (third quotation), p. 21 (fourth quotation).

38. *Corpus Christi Caller Times*, December 23, 1883; King, *Great South*, p. 111 (first quotation); and "A Tour through Texas," *New Monthly Magazine* 131 (1864): 245 (second quotation).

39. "Internal Improvements in Texas," *De Bow's Review* 6 (1848): 364–65; "Resources and Progress of Texas," *De Bow's Review* 4 (1847): 319; "Texas Lands," *De Bow's Review* 8 (1850): 63–65; and "On Gulf States and the Amazon," *De Bow's Review* 18 (1855): 91–93.

High plateaus and mountains in West Texas supported sheep, and San Antonio was clarioned as an outlet for woolen goods. That city was the gateway for cattle, too. Innumerable herds, "happier and prettier than ever was pastured by Virgil in his pastorals," enlivened the western plains.

Naturally, the interior, rolling priaire was the finest section of all — a Golden Mean within the golden mean. An entry in *De Bow's* in the mid-1850s described an almost "wanton waste of nature" in the Brazos Valley. "For many miles around the cotton, corn, and every other vegetable substance seem to overload the earth"; obese-looking hogs, plump corn, and huge, orange-colored pumpkins demonstrated the soil's fertility. To the north, also in this intermediate region along the upper Trinity River and the Red River, lay the grain lands, where wheat, rye, and other small grains grew as well as in any place in Missouri. Nobody could doubt that Texas was destined to become "one of the brightest stars of the American Constellation."[40]

The capital city of Austin, positioned centrally on the break of slope between the western mountain zone and the blackland prairie, was also included in the Golden Mean. There one could find "the wild hunter of the plains and the shrewd businessman of the coast side by side in friendly discourse." Early resident George Bonnell, whose name was given to a hilltop overlooking present-day Lake Austin, likened the town to "the ancient City of Rome" built on seven hills. William Bollaert visited the tiny capital in 1843 and, despite finding it unkempt and virtually abandoned because of the threat from Mexico, employed the same classical analogy as Bonnell but was more precise: "If Rome was celebrated in song for her 'seven hills,' Austin may boast of her 'thousand mounds.'" Bollaert was struck by the aesthetic character of Austin's location, claiming that the city's beauty equaled "the Arcadian groves" and was unsurpassed by any other place in North America. Like Edward Stiff, this Englishman saw emigration "propelling the car of enterprise to the West" and believed that the wild, little-known country beyond Austin would be redeemed by industry and commerce. Such a tract, full of pastoral phrases and romantic appeal, was intended to attract settlement. Bollaert anticipated a mineral industry, viticulture, and river traf-

---

40. "Texas — Her Natural Advantages — Wool and Factories," *De Bow's Review* 10 (1851): 464; "Agriculture Capacities of Western Texas," *De Bow's Review* 18 (1855): 54–55; and "Texas — Its Resources, Lands, Rivers, Products, Etc.," *De Bow's Review* 9 (1850): 195–97.

fic with Austin as their hub. And although his visit came at an un-
propitious time, what he saw pleased both himself and others to whom
he reported in England.[41]

Architecture and Missions

Not much remains of early Hispanic architecture in Texas. Some people, like Bollaert, found similarities to Palestine in the appearance of
houses with courtyards, tropical plants, and traditional mud brick and
white-washed stone buildings. These architectural forms reflected Mediterranean styles that coped with sunlight, temperature, and air circulation. Hispanic architecture borrowed these "round-arched, rhythmic and
fun loving" styles from the Old World, colored tiles and adobe were
adjustments from Mexico, and flat roofs west of the Pecos River, in New
Mexico and Arizona, reflected a desert quality that typified pueblo features. Spanish houses in Texas were adapted to site and exposure. People built them to last, using local materials that gave them distinctive
textures and colors.[42]

Turn-of-the-twentieth-century enthusiasts for these Mediterranean
styles were equally impressed by their cultural implications. One of them
reminded readers that when the Jamestown Colony was only an infant,
Spanish settlements existed in Florida and New Mexico. Spanish explorers had conquered the New World interior from Kansas to Buenos
Aires.[43]

San Antonio was the center of this special cultural mix and it sustained the Mediterranean motif. Like Austin, it had the advantage of
being centrally located, "an old man basking in the sun on the principal crossroads of Texas." The Hispanic west and south met Anglo east
and north. San Antonio was nearer to Mexico City than it was to Knox-
ville or Atlanta and was almost as close to Guatemala City as it was to
Chicago.

The city was also the spiritual capital of the Southwest. San Antonio's

41. George W. Bonnell, *Topographical Description of Texas*, p. 65; and W. Eugene
Hollon and Ruth L. Butler, eds., *William Bollaert's Texas*, pp. 194–99.
42. Willard B. Robinson, *Gone from Texas: Our Lost Architectural Heritage*, pp. 24–
28; Rexford Newcomb, *The Spanish House for America*, p. 14 (quotation); and idem,
Mediterranean Domestic Architecture in the United States, pp. [2–4], 157–60.
43. Charles F. Lummis, *The Spanish Pioneers*, p. 23.

missions were older than those in California by almost a hundred years. The first religious center in Texas, in Corpus Christi de la Isleta near El Paso, dated back to 1682 and showed the usual adobe familiar to Spanish colonists. When B. Butler Harris passed through in 1849 en route to California, he admired the town's single-story adobe houses and the atmosphere of Old Spain.[44]

Presidios, as places of fortification and protection, followed plans for similar bastions in Renaissance Europe. The size, arrangement, and entire geometry of town planning, with the plaza as the geographical center of urban life, reflected ordinances from the time of King Philip II in 1573. Spanish settlement types, styles, and ways of life naturally dominated this far-flung outpost until the period of *empresario* landholdings and Texas independence.[45]

The Texas Revolution resulted in intense conflict and hatred, especially in the strip between the Nueces River and the Rio Grande, where Spanish-speaking ranchers retreated or were forced out. Contrasts between an old Hispanic aristocracy—the urban elite and politically powerful of San Antonio—and Mexican campesinos became blurred as mutual antagonism, lawlessness, and violence marked the clash between a traditional, largely pastoral Hispanic economy and the new agricultural and expansionist Anglo one. Roy Bedichek has made the interesting comment that the prefix "Mexican" has been used in Texas for anything small or stunted. The "Mexican eagle," or caracara, is a "degenerate" bird not really an eagle; so are the "Mexican walnut" and "Mexican apple" trees. In contrast, the term "Indian" denotes beauty and color, as in the Indian paintbrush flower or color pink, and "Spanish" suggests grace, as in hanging moss.[46]

Be that as it may, the cultural legacy of Spain and New Spain has remained uncontested in place-names, plants, and animals of the Southwest. Forty-one of the 254 counties in Texas have Spanish names. Rivers with Hispanic names abound throughout the state, as do city and street names. H. L. Mencken recalled the rich vocabulary ranging from rancho, mustang, sombrero, poncho, and corral, typifying horsemanship, right through physical geography, exemplified by canyon, sierra, mesa, and

---

44. Green Peyton, *San Antonio: City in the Sun,* p. 2 (quotation), 264; Robinson, *Gone from Texas,* p. 8; and Benjamin Butler Harris, *The Gila Trail: Texas Argonauts and the California Gold Rush,* p. 51.

45. Zelia Nuttall, "Royal Ordinances Concerning the Laying Out of New Towns," *Hispanic American Historical Review* 4 (1921): 743–45.

46. Roy Bedichek, *Adventures with a Texas Naturalist,* pp. 220–22, 272.

tornado. Such words mirrored the unconscious, authentic incorporation of Hispanic elements into the geography of land and life.[47]

It is interesting that early on it was Italy, an idealized, classical civilization of imperial greatness, that writers promoted, not the actual, tangible Spanish and Mexican aspects of Texas, which spoke so much more forcefully and naturally to the Mediterranean metaphor. Rather than acknowledge and admire such Hispanic roots in Texas, boosters talked about an idealized Mediterranean, intended for the consumption of non-Latin people. They promoted a romantic Mediterranean of sunlight and blue skies under which peasant villages thrived, in order to attract immigrants and sustain new settlement. They structured the image to make Texas into something that an alien culture could possess and control. Accent was placed on the state's peculiar geography, crops, and settlement morphology and served to differentiate Texas from similar regions in the South. Only Florida shared in many of the same tropical products until the entire Mediterranean image was co-opted by the agricultural and intellectual prowess of a burgeoning California, where it has since remained.

47. Gerald Ashford, *Spanish Texas: Yesterday and Today*, pp. 3–4.

6. Mirages:
Foreign Views of Texas

The image of Texas as a beautiful parkland, natural garden, or Italy served to attract and stimulate foreign immigration. Individually, authors and correspondents communicated these ideas to friends, families, and to their readers. A number of publications by Kennedy and by German commentators underscored opportunities for prosperity among their countrymen. There was a living to be made in Texas, and not only was life profitable, but it could also be happy and contented. How did these images "play" abroad? Did people enthusiastically adopt and repeat them to others, or did they greet them with disbelief or disdain?

A good deal is known about the activities of German agents and their associates in promoting movement into the Texas Hill Country on the eastern flanks of the Edwards Plateau. British enterprise in Texas is less talked about. Although few actual organized attempts at landing groups of British settlers took place, a good many Scots and English settlers came in as families or one by one from areas further east; and the Irish figured in *empresario* schemes. As foreign commercial and political interest in Texas grew, the British public became more aware of that exotic region some six thousand miles away in the American subtropics.

Public interest in Britain concerning Texas involved two issues. The first was the problem of annexation in the late 1830s and early 1840s when a dozen or so books debated the questions of political recognition and international commerce with the young Republic. Slavery was a central concern. The second involved opportunities for investments by capitalists in the western rangelands of Texas after the Civil War. Livestock proved a magnet for investors, who speculated in wild long-horn cattle and later in improved cattle breeds as demands for meat grew in America and Europe. Some aristocrats and well-to-do members of the middle class sent their sons to manage landholdings in Texas. Young people seized by the spirit of adventure and the opportunity for excitement on the open ranges of the American Southwest also emigrated. Some of them hired themselves out as trail drivers, cowhands, and hunters on the High Plains.

Blight in the Garden

Much of the literature from the 1830s and 1840s that celebrated the garden image called for husbandry and enterprise and rested on a few firsthand accounts from authors such as Holley, Lawrence, Kenedy, Ikin, and Muir. Britishers who promoted Texas, like Edward, Kennedy, and Ikin, received favorable attention from national newspapers and periodicals. But there were other authors who called the whole Texas adventure a hoax and who, after short stints in the Republic, returned to England to recount their experiences and discourage emigration. Such authors intended to cure "Texas fever" by detailing horror stories and sensational accounts of what "real" life was like on the frontier. This conflicting testimony about conditions in the young Republic confused Britain's reading public. Among the "amazing number" of publications between 1837 and 1847 dealing with Texas, two books in particular sought to counter favorable reports from Kennedy and others and scoffed at the idea of Texas as a garden. Both publications deprecated the quality of the Republic's land, resources, and inhabitants.[1]

N. Doran Maillard landed in Galveston, merely an "inhabitable sandbank," he sneered, on January 30, 1840. He departed six months later, having traveled widely up and down the coast, writing for the *Richmond Telescope* and becoming a member of the Texas Bar. Maillard's history indicted Texans for "inhumane" treatment of slaves and Indians and warned the British government about racketeers and land agents.

---

1. Mary Lee Spence, "British Impressions of Texas and Texans," *Southwestern Historical Quarterly* 70 (1966): 163–83. See also Thomas W. Cutrer, *The English Texans*.

He sought especially to prevent immigrants from throwing away their lives by moving to Texas. His 512-page diatribe, published in London in 1842, attacked both the place and its people by concentrating on four points.[2]

First, sudden weather changes, notably in spring, precipitated the onset of agues. Summer heat with temperatures of 125° F, he exaggerated, followed by the stormy weather and severe cold of winter, made tillage exceptionally difficult for those few who survived such climatic extremes. Maillard singled out Mary Austin Holley, whom he named "gentle shepherdess," for spreading extravagant and seductive falsehoods about a beneficent climate and good health in Texas. She had deceived readers, as had Kennedy. Although others may have been taken in by the latter's Irish blustering, Maillard knew from his sojourn that Texas was the "Bog of Allen of America," not the "Italy" described by such promoters.

The second issue involved "land sharks" who tried to dupe potential emigrants in the United Kingdom, or who preyed heavily on newly arrived and naive settlers in Texas. Third, Maillard warned that British immigrants could be conscripted to fight against Mexico. Finally, he noted the absence of dependable specie; promissory or Treasury notes were worthless, Maillard claimed.[3]

Maillard's book fairly "roasted" Texas and Texans. He glossed over the existence of excellent cotton crops, electing to emphasize that the lands that grew them were wet places where alligators, snakes, scorpions, and galley nippers waited to pounce on fair English skins. This kind of invective did not pass unchallenged. Bollaert objected strenuously to charges of inhospitality. But Maillard's book heaped fuel on the fire of controversy about what was real and what was imaginary in Texas.[4]

A much slimmer volume by Charles Hooton also dismissed the Texas Garden as a chimera. He opened his account by saying that he "had the misfortune to visit Texas in hope" and returned with "hope deferred." He joined a shipload of thirty British settlers who took three months to make the crossing from London to Galveston, where they arrived in March, 1841, after grounding and narrowly escaping shipwreck on the sandbar. Much of Hooton's time was passed in a two-room hut on Galveston's outskirts to which mice, rats, cats, and mud daubers had com-

2. N. Doran Maillard, *The History of the Republic of Texas*, pp. iv, 354.
3. Ibid., pp. 313 (first quotation), 319 (second quotation), 350–52.
4. Spence, "British Impressions," p. 172.

plete access. Free-ranging hogs rooted up the few vegetables he managed to coerce from the sandy garden.[5]

Hooton's 1847 book offered a valuable antidote to promotional tracts. He explained how people invariably tend to become enthusiastic about foreign countries like Texas, New Zealand, or Australia, considering them to be poetic and romantic retreats. Actual experiences usually dash such high expectations, particularly when travelers reach foreign regions more undeveloped than their own. Quite understandably, therefore, Texas appeared niggardly, unkempt, and rude to British and other immigrants, said Hooton, and he blamed newspapers and publicists for cashing in on hopes for a better life. He condemned Texas newspapers as a miserable mélange of plagiarized clippings and editorial drivel whose publishers included notices of marriages only for the cake and whisky they commanded. Promoters of Texas back in England were no more honest, he added. He piously explained that his book of recollections about his nine-month stay would prevent settlement and not "betray the Northern immigrant to almost inevitable ruin and death," as previous books about Texas had done.[6]

Galveston and its environs provided the first and greatest shock to the hopeful immigrant. Never had a place appeared so gloomy, unhealthy, or miserable: "a mere lazar-house for disease and death to revel in," was the charge. What had appeared as white marble from the ship as it made its approach turned out to be peeling whitewash on the walls of a few wooden huts. That false image of Galveston symbolized all of Texas for Hooton, who noted that not one of his thirty shipmates settled successfully; most of them scattered inland, moved to the United States, returned to England, or died in Texas within a year.

Health was the problem. Immigrants from Britain had no notions about dealing with tropical sicknesses. They had no effective medicines to treat the miasmatic complaints to which their bodies were unused. Hooton narrated a series of poignant vignettes about families who succumbed to fevers and to plagues of biting insects. Most of the populace lived on the coastal plain, he noted, and therefore suffered greatly from such endemic agues. He lambasted Lawrence and Kennedy in particular for penning rosy accounts about distant places like Austin and "west" Texas while ignoring the problems of finding potable water and ade-

5. Charles Hooton, *St. Louis' Isle, or Texiana*, pp. 1 (quotation), 44, 49–50.
6. Ibid., pp. 11, 14 (quotation).

quate food in and around Galveston — the first stop for so many. In addition, he provided vivid details about the coarse habits of Texans, who expectorated and cursed with impunity and who resorted to the Bowie knife to settle disputes, reflecting a general disregard for the rule of law.[7]

How did such contradictory statements affect public and government confidence in Texas? Maillard, Hooton, and three or four other British authors in the 1830s and 1840s rejected both the Mediterranean garden motif and the idea of home. They sought to lampoon the images that American writers and their British counterparts, exemplified by Bollaert, Falconer, Houstoun, and, of course, the redoubtable Kennedy, had done so much to build.

One way of assessing the popularity of these various images of Texas is to examine newspapers and journals in the United Kingdom to see whose side they took. Another is to refer to official and diplomatic correspondence. The British government, through its secretary of state, Lord Palmerston, was very much interested in the Texas question from both a political and economic standpoint. The government needed hard facts from reliable observers and consulted Texas officials and diplomats such as Ashbel Smith, who usually calmed fears and refuted negative comments. Texans abroad helped to mitigate the tendentiousness, but not the confusion, caused by Maillard and Hooton.

From the mid-1830s until the Civil War, a hodgepodge of British journalists, promoters, scientists, soldiers, politicians, and sportsmen traveled to America and wrote books or articles about the young nation. Most of them came from middle-class backgrounds, and almost every one of the 230 or so who published accounts had a different reason for making the journey and writing about it. Most travelers' views were reinforced by their experiences; in other words, they saw what they wanted to see, and what they witnessed tended to impress them, especially the material well-being and promise of such a huge continent. Many travelers advised would-be immigrant readers to move quickly westward from New York, the disembarkation point, into the farm belt in Indiana, Illinois, and later Iowa, where soils were fertile and relatively cheap. Authors explained that taxes were generally low and household goods and trade equipment entered free of duty. Many of them also commended social égalité in the States. People could make something of themselves without undue regard for birth and breeding. But

7. Ibid., pp. 7, 26, 33.

most of these authors knew about Texas only by secondhand reports.[8] Texas was off the beaten track for these popularizers. They recognized as time passed that emigration was not merely for adventurers or indigents, but also for families of sobriety and wealth. In this respect, Texas was not initially attractive because the Southwest and Trans-Mississippi vastness in general appeared too difficult to reach and too dangerous to live in. In sum, once the traveler, let alone the emigrant wishing to establish roots, proceeded west from New Orleans, he or she was committed to true adventure. Naturally, railroads changed this situation, but initially overland progress by coach and riverboat as far as New Orleans was tortuous and lengthy. To relinquish that last bastion of civilization by heading off into Texas was risky and probably foolhardy.

British authors who did experience Texas or knew a good deal about conditions tended to make slavery a major concern, especially in regard to foreign recognition and possible annexation by the United States. Because of this social issue and its economic ramifications, and because Texas was so different in terms of its history, location, and size, those writers who made deprecatory remarks about going to North America chose Texas as a *cause célèbre*. A thirty-six page article in London's *Quarterly Review* for 1838, which acknowledged the works of Holley, Parker, and William E. Channing, reproved Texans for declaring independence from Mexico and subverting that nation's policy against slavery.[9]

The British public was bombarded with similar tracts about political instability and about tolerance of slavery in Texas during the early 1840s. Rancorous correspondence appeared in *The Times* in 1841, when Richard Hartnel attacked Kennedy's optimistic vision of Texas as "more like poetry than fact." Hartnel strongly urged that Britain withhold recognition of the Republic because many British investors who had funds tied up in Mexico would undoubtedly suffer. Hartnel's correspondence was bound in a book and served to draw attention to that region where "fruits of a tropical climate [grew] side by side with those of Europe." The financial difficulties of British investors did not detract, however, from his admission that Texas had soils of "extraordinary fertility," but Kennedy had been much too fulsome in his praise.[10]

8. Max Berger, *The British Traveller in America, 1836–1860*, pp. 13–14, 178–83; and Jane L. Mesick, *The English Traveller in America, 1785–1835*, pp. 4–5.

9. "The Texas," *Quarterly Review* 61 (1838): 326–62.

10. Richard Hartnel, comp., *Texas and California*, pp. 16, 30 (first quotation), 22 (second quotation).

Propagandist opinions surfaced in support of Kennedy. *The Times* (June 12, 1841) approved of his *Texas* book. The *Manchester Guardian* ran quite glowing excerpts from Texas travelers between 1837 and 1841, and *Chamber's Edinburgh Journal* (1837, 1843), *The Illustrated London News* (1842), and the prestigious *Journal of the Royal Geographic Society* all published essays describing the advantages and opportunities for settlers.[11]

A fascinating account of the Galveston area by Percy Bolingbroke St. John, who opposed Hooton, appeared in *Campbell's Foreign Semi-Monthly Magazine* (1843). This son of literary figure Augustus St. John visited Texas in 1842 and published several essays about his experiences. Later he translated Aimard's popular "Indian Tales," many of which were set in Texas, into English.

St. John's article involved a hunting excursion. Clothed in a Peruvian poncho, sou'wester hat, pantaloons, jacket, and sturdy boots, the author and six companions sailed across Galveston Bay loaded with guns, shot, powder, "fixings" for a tent, water, biscuits, salt, butter, coffee, several bottles of American whisky, and, most important of all, ample tobacco.[12]

Working up close to shore in a thick mist, the party beached in Edward's Bay and set off to "walk into the ducks." Eleven ducks and two geese soon fell to volleys of swan shot; later a blazing fire, duck stew, fine tobacco, and drink drew St. John into a reverie about "Father Thames" back home. He admitted savoring this new life, with its dash and exotic flavor. He received a further surprise from an encounter with Esther, a sort of leatherstocking whom one of his party knew. Widow Esther lived near Galveston Bay and was also English. The compatriots talked and smoked together, then she demonstrated the art of a night "fire" hunt. Using blazing pine knots to make the deer's eyes glow, she shot a doe at about fifty paces. The attractive widow with her four youngsters, recalled St. John, preferred this simple life on the frontier — a special contrast with Hooton's account of another English widow in Galveston who lived off the hospitality and generosity of the city's suitors before slighting them all by hurriedly departing. St. John wrote enthusiastically about Texas, and his stories contain both drama and accurate detail.[13]

11. Spence, "British Impressions," pp. 169–75.

12. Percy Bolingbroke St. John, "Bentley's Miscellany," *Campbell's Foreign Semi-Monthly Magazine* 4 (1843): 510–16.

13. Ibid., pp. 7, 11–13.

British literature expressed doubts about Texas. It was a remote, distinct, English-speaking region totally beyond the jurisdiction of the home government. In spite of barbs from Maillard and Hooton, there was no doubt that abundant, varied resources beckoned stout-hearted farmers. British colonists, it was generally felt, were less capable of exploiting them than were their American brothers and sisters. Difficulties in travel and adjustment tended to discourage most except the most adventurous and thoroughly curious.

Popular Literature and Texas

Writers like the young traveler St. John capitalized on a tradition in American letters that Europeans found fascinating, a tradition that traced back to James Fenimore Cooper. This American luminary's novels of frontier life, Indians, and the progress of settlement grew immensely popular in Western Europe, particularly in Germany, in the 1830s and 1840s. Elderly Johann Wolfgang von Goethe admired Cooper and drew on his *Pioneers* and similar tales in the 1820s for plans to develop stories about emigrants in America. Frenchman Gustave Aimard, whose work St. John translated into English, and the prolific German novelist Friedrich Strubberg likewise spun out tales of adventure in the American West, often concentrating on Texas.

By 1800 almost nine hundred works about America had been published in Germany, and between 1815 and 1850, an additional fifty or so travel accounts appeared. Many novels pursued the theme of confrontation between civilization and savagery on the frontier, one of Cooper's most popular themes abroad. An important source of information about the West came from a "half-dozen German-born traveller-novelists whose personal lives and literary production form one of the most colorful chapters in the history of German letters."[14] Friedrich Gerstacker, Otto Ruppius, Baldwin Mollhausen, Friedrich Strubberg, and Karl Postl (alias Charles Sealsfield) presented a formidable library of talent. All of them and their imitators owed a debt to Cooper, especially to his leatherstocking characters, whom they frequently dressed

14. D. L. Ashliman, "The Novel of Western Adventure in Nineteenth-Century Germany," *Western American Literature* 3 (1968): 133–45; and Preston A. Barba, "Cooper in Germany," *German American Annals* 12 (1914): 3–60.

up as German immigrants. Such fictitious frontiersmen were invariably well educated, medically expert, and well read. Based on "personal experience," these books represented lifelike and authentic reading to a European public that eagerly purchased them.[15]

Friedrich Armand Strubberg (1806–1889), who penned fifty-seven novels under the pseudonym "Armand," drew from a prolonged stay on the frontier in German Texas. He came to Texas as "Dr. F. Shubbert" in 1844 and settled on the San Gabriel River. Strubberg possibly knew William Bollaert and had read Kennedy's *Texas,* which probably influenced his decision to choose Texas. In 1846, at the behest of the Baron Otto von Meusebach, Strubberg agreed to assist in founding the settlement of Fredericksburg. But he moved to Arkansas two years later, embittered with his treatment by von Meusebach, and finally returned to Kassel, Germany. His sister Emilie encouraged his literary bent, so that in 1858, at the age of fifty-two, Strubberg began to publish the first of his many novels about life in the American West, particularly Texas.[16]

His first book transports the reader to the Leona River, an imaginary tributary of the Rio Grande, where he and three German colonists settled in a stockade. Experts in German-American Romantic literature have praised Strubberg's work for its color, accuracy, and realism, and for his sympathetic understanding and treatment of Indians. His chief interest in this first work, and in many others, is hunting. Czar, a white stallion, and Trust, his faithful hound, accompany Armand on various frontier sorties. He shoots deer and bison, endures stampedes, prairie fires, and several brushes with hostile Indians (usually Comanches) while camping in the vast outdoors.[17]

Strubberg's novels portrayed a primitive, unsullied Texas upon which settlement and progress were advancing. The author's physical stature and his attire back in Germany reflected this literary genre. He sported a flowing moustache and a black band over a once-infected eye, and a theatrical cloak covered his tall, massive frame. He looked like the

15. Barba, "Cooper in Germany," p. 135; and Paul C. Weber, *America in Imaginative German Literature in the First Half of the Nineteenth Century,* pp. 120–55, 152–56, 226–30.

16. Preston A. Barba, *The Life and Works of Friedrich Armand Strubberg;* and Armin O. Huber, "Frederic Armand Strubberg, Alias Dr. Shubbert, Town-Builder, Physician, and Adventurer, 1806–1889," *West Texas Historical Association Yearbook* 38 (1962): 37–71.

17. Barba, *Strubberg,* pp. 7–8, 18; and C. F. Lascelles Wraxall, ed., *The Backwoodsman; or, Life on the Indian Frontier,* pp. 6, 12–14, 18, 22, 43, 50, 107, passim.

flamboyant traveler and explorer that he was, and readers found his straightforward, lively prose and action-packed stories exciting.

An 1859 book provides useful historical documentation concerning German colonies in Texas. It introduces readers to the Werner family, whose plight and tragic circumstances reflected the brutal conditions of the trek inland to New Braunfels. *Friedricksburg* (1867) completed the account of a German plantation, combining faithful documentation with literary form. Strubberg became colonial director of this daughter settlement to New Braunfels and penned a colorful account of life there, including encounters with both friendly and hostile Indians.[18]

Like similar writers of popular literature, including Sealsfield and May, Strubberg paid close attention to the dress and customs of Indians. They assumed three basic roles toward whites in his books: first, they appeared aggressive and hostile; second, they became more friendly; and third, they grew increasingly bewildered by the transformation and loss of lands. His fictitious Indians were a proud, handsome, primitive people who were prepared to befriend settlers; but they were also doomed to extinction. The sudden, often surprising appearances of Indians in his novels reflect the pathos of changing conditions, and Strubberg's readers knew that they would not survive; nature was good, but an alien, intrusive culture was defiling it.[19]

Strubberg's prolific writings both supported and reflected the reading public's fascination for North America's frontier. In the 1830s, almost 150,000 people sailed from Germany to America, and in the three years after 1844 more than 7,000 German emigrants landed in Texas. Such long-distance travel influenced German literature, which responded to this interest with stories and anecdotes about conditions in North America.

Another writer about Texas, Charles Sealsfield (the pseudonym used by Karl Postl), recounted his experiences, too. This novelist's principal character, Nathan, was an epic figure—a Boone-like figure in Texas representing the notion of both "fearless" squatter and "honest" pioneer. Correspondents picked up similar generalizations, reminding friends and relatives back home that prosperity could be won from the land

18. Barba, *Strubberg,* pp. 21–25.

19. Preston A. Barba, "The American Indian in German Fiction," *German American Annals* 15 (1913): 143–74, especially pp. 158–59; and Lewis H. Brereton, "American Indians of the Southeast and Southwest in the Works of Charles Sealsfield, Karl May and Friedrich Armand Strubberg," pp. 37–38, 71, 73.

by courage, perseverance, and initiative. They told stories about hunting, beelining, and fending off Indians in the quest to harvest new crops and secure a future.[20]

English readers, on the other hand, were comparing Texas with the other outlets for young men in the British Empire. An author in *Sidney's Emigrant's Journal* (1850) wrote of German colonists in Texas and explained away their problems as being due to the climate that was "dangerous and destructive" to northern constitutions. In particular, the coast had a "fatal" climate and the sugar lands in the lower Brazos River Valley resembled the "jungles of India." Much of the rolling country inland was better, however, and from the Guadalupe River to the Rio Grande there existed a dry grassland, excellent for sheep, which was very similar to interior Australia and to South Africa's Cape Colony.[21]

A "Letter from Texas" in *Sidney's* provided a vivid description of several "wild western men," heavily armed and dressed in ponchos or blanket coats, huddled around log fires in an Austin barroom. These "heroes of the Texas struggle" with "old earthen pipes, with stems of yellow reeds" poked into sallow faces, talked of the Mexican campaign, of the Alamo, the death of Colonel Crockett, and about fighting Comanches. They did not talk of agriculture or land improvement, but of fights; even hunting, the usual topic, was generally ignored. The English visitor who penned the story had never met such men before and was impressed by their courteous, self-confident, unpretentious manners. They had "an inner dignity and mental remoteness," he explained, that came from lives of trial and danger. The rough Texans, wearing big black felt hats, were civil but absolutely independent.[22]

One evening a mountain man and his followers entered the bar. He was clothed in deerskins with "mocassins worked over the instep in the most approved style of fashion," wore a long Bowie knife in a gaudy sheath, and carried a large-bore, heavy rifle. His stories of California excited the locals, "who like most western men, are always inquiring

20. Preston A. Barba, "Emigration as Reflected in German Fiction," *German American Annals* 12 (1914): 193–227, especially p. 194; Selma M. Raunick, "A Survey of German Literature in Texas," *Southwestern Historical Quarterly* 33 (1929): 134–59; and Terry G. Jordan and Marlis A. Jordan, eds., "Letters of a German Pioneer in Texas," *Southwestern Historical Quarterly* 69 (1966): 463–72.

21. "Letters Describing a Ride through Texas," *Sidney's Emigrant's Journal and Traveller's Magazine*, pp. 1 (first and second quotations), 4 (third quotation).

22. "Letters from Texas," *Sidney's Emigrant's Journal* 5, p. 1.

what there is 'farther west,' and always disposed to move to some El Dorado."[23]

On balance, however, the account concluded, "to the poor emigrant who sighs for a spot of land," Canada's fertile soils, despite its hard winters, "are far more likely to realize his hopes than cheaper land under the enervating sun of Texas." A voyage of many weeks was necessary to reach this far-flung Texas land, and on arrival the newcomer came up against a barrier of sickness. In such an adopted land "there is a greater risk to life than in any British Colony," concluded the author. It was a good place for lovers of tropical agriculture and slavery and for people who wanted an "indolent, half-barbarian life in a country abounding with game." But for the average Britisher in pursuit of a new life, Texas was far from the garden paradise described by its promotors.[24]

Diplomats Speak

British officials tended to agree that fellow nationals were generally ill-equipped to compete with other Europeans on such a rigorous, distant frontier. One diplomat noted that his countrymen "make but sorry work of it in taming the wilds, compared with the American races." Kennedy, who became Her Majesty's consul in Galveston, wrote in 1844 that prior to his time only a handful of British emigrants had landed in that port city. On the other hand, several hundred Europeans, mainly from France and Germany, had endured the long sea voyage. The Irish flourished in Galveston under the jurisdiction of the French Catholic bishop Odin. French settlers, however, managed poorly, soon becoming "barbarized" when isolated or in small numbers.[25]

Kennedy warned against buying land titles in Europe, where speculators were hawking Texas scrip for one English shilling an acre shortly after the Declaration of Independence. Kennedy welcomed younger, stronger, wealthier British settlers who were prepared to undertake manual labor in clearing land for a farm. They should not snap

23. Ibid., p. 6.
24. "Letters Describing a Ride through Texas," pp. 1 (first and second quotations), 2 (third quotation), 4 (fourth quotation).
25. Elliot to Addington, March 26, 1843, in Ephraim D. Admas, ed., *British Diplomatic Correspondence Concerning the Republic of Texas, 1838–1846*, p. 168; and Kennedy to Aberdeen, September 9, 1844, in ibid., p. 357.

up cheap bottomlands, nor occupy other areas along the coast, he insisted. As far as 150 miles inland such places were fever-ridden. Kennedy preferred lands in the "West," beyond the Colorado River, and he stressed that immigrants must ask themselves whether they were fitted for the country, not whether the country was fitted for them. In that regard, European governments owed settlers a precise, detailed, and true account of conditions.[26]

This honest exchange of ideas with the home government reflects concern about image and reality. The reports of Francis C. Sheridan, a diplomatic colleague of Kennedy's stationed in Barbados, also focused on this issue. In his capacity as colonial secretary under Sir Evan John Murray MacGregor, governor of the Windward Islands, Sheridan sailed to Galveston in December, 1839, to prepare an eyewitness report for Lord Palmerston and Britain's political establishment about possible recognition of Texas. His dispatch, dated July 12, 1840, may have provided Palmerston with information needed to negotiate treaties with the Republic. Sheridan's report and his personal journal offer useful insights into his own interests and observations and into the sorts of questions raised by his superiors.[27]

Sheridan observed that "false and flaming accounts given of Texas" at home and abroad had generated mischief and misinformation. The British public should place little stock in such accounts, he added, which amounted to boosterism and gimmicks to sell lands. His official dispatch confirmed that Texas soils were extraordinarily fertile. Cotton lands grew three times more than equivalent soils in Georgia and the Carolinas, and more than in Louisiana or Mississippi. He wrote that "Texas may challenge the World to show richer and more productive soils," but he disagreed with claims about the mildness and salubrity of its climate. Sheridan disliked the weather and also coastal ports such as Velasco and Galveston. The interior, upland region was better suited for U.K. farmers, he believed, especially for sheep raisers. Emigrants to these northern parts would soon become "the Yeomanry of the Texas Country," without a need for slaves, who worked cotton and sugar plantations on the unhealthy coast.[28]

26. Kennedy to Aberdeen, ibid., pp. 357–61.

27. Willis W. Pratt, ed., *Galveston Island; or, A Few Months Off the Coast of Texas: The Journal of Francis C. Sheridan, 1839–1840*; and Adams, *British Diplomatic Correspondence*, pp. 18–26.

28. Pratt, *Galveston Island*, pp. 43, 141; and Adams, *British Diplomatic Correspondence*, p. 19.

Sheridan thus gave qualified support for British settlers, adding that Texans who had been rebuffed by the United States over the annexation question would welcome people from the Old Country. The extra British hands would also help in resolving the issue of slavery, making such repugnant labor unnecessary. But Sheridan had his doubts concerning the settlement enterprise in Texas. Although he supported the break with Mexico, he worried about how people would "dispose of the Booty." He had class-conscious disdain for the character and social mores of the populace and for alleged swindlers and frequent violent crimes.[29] Texas together with much of North America received typical condescension from the British well-to-do.

French Connections

Unlike their more conservative European cousins, French-born or French-speaking entrepreneurs, travelers, and intellectuals committed to utopian socialism found Texas irresistible. Théodore-Frédéric Gaillardet, a respected journalist and writer, popularized Texas in France and promoted the young Republic in official circles. He accompanied Alphonse de Saligny, secretary of the French embassy in Washington, on a visit to Texas in 1839. Gaillardet was most impressed by the plenitude of natural resources and unlimited economic potential of Texas and urged the French government to recognize the new nation's sovereignty and independence.

Gaillardet loved the climate and fertile land whose "green carpet decorated with wild flowers" lasted most of the year. "It is a garden," he exclaimed. "Nature alone is sufficient to reproduce the treasures of this vast park in which every adornment and every fruit of the earth grew without cultivation." He concluded ebulliently that "Americans call Texas their Italy."[30]

It was the promise of this other "Italy" as a desirable physical backdrop that drew efforts to create French-style communities committed to fraternal and egalitarian principles after 1840. In that year, the French government concluded a treaty with Texas, becoming the first nation to recognize the Republic.

29. Pratt, *Galveston Island*, p. 18.
30. Théodore F. Gaillardet, *Sketches of Early Texas and Louisiana*, pp. 62–63.

The first test of utopian principles in Texas came from Etienne Cabet's "Icarians," named after Icarus, the Greek god. In January, 1848, Cabet made his pronouncement, "C'est au Texas!" which he based on advice and encouragement from British socialist philosopher Robert Owen, who at one time wished to make in Texas a communistic community.[31]

Land agents of the Peters colony drew up a contract for a huge tract of land, subsequently much reduced in size, along the Red River, and in March, 1848, the first of Cabet's advance guard disembarked in New Orleans and prepared to take possession of the grant. The sixty-nine French settlers sailed up the Red River to Shreveport, then struck out on foot with a few carts to carry possessions. They headed toward the wilderness site two hundred miles away, eventually stopping near present-day Justin in Denton County, where living conditions quickly deteriorated. Sickness, poor food, feelings of isolation, and ignorance about conditions made what looked beautiful in June when they first arrived appear intolerable and oppressive in July and August. After a few months, the experiment began to collapse and survivors straggled back to Shreveport. The Red River utopia proved a mirage, however, for Cabet, who came to New Orleans and then headed off into Illinois to continue his experiment. He blamed imprudence on the part of his first colonists and the few who joined them for the failure of his dream in Texas.[32]

In 1855, Victor Prosper Considérant arrived with a small group of idealists to form a new order, again in North Texas. A dedicated socialist, Considérant had journeyed to America in 1852 and saw in Texas the right place for his experiment in communal living. "The landscape was classic and charming," he explained. "Nature has done all." The land around the small town of Dallas seemed excellent for wine making and the practice of horticulture. It was abundant, cheap, and situated in a southern latitude away from harsher temperatures. On his return to France, Considérant published details of his plan in *Au Texas;* he formed a company, sent agents to purchase land, and encouraged his countrymen and others to join the enterprise. The settlement of La Reunion would be a grand success.[33]

From the beginning, the settlement encountered difficulties. Con-

31. Albert Shaw, *Icaria: A Chapter in the History of Communism;* and Ernest G. Fischer, *Marxists and Utopias in Texas,* pp. 127–31.

32. Shaw, *Icaria,* pp. 33, 35, 38–39.

33. William Hammond and Margaret Hammond, *La Reunion: A French Settlement in Texas,* pp. 39–41.

sidérant's people were mostly artists and better-educated Europeans unused to harsh conditions and hard manual labor. Few farmers were among
the "sabot-shod, pantalooned, weary travellers" who entered Dallas in
June, 1855, after a six-week trek from Houston. The city welcomed them
and watched them mark out a thirty-eight-acre townsite and establish
small gardens, plots for horticulture, and larger fields for grains around
the crude log and stone houses. But not many English-speaking Texans,
whom Gaillardet called the "loamy fertile outflow of the Anglo-Saxon
race," joined in the project to provide the expertise that the French utopians so sorely lacked.[34]

As the year progressed, misfortune, personal rivalries, petty jealousies,
and ignorance about cultivation methods dogged the infant community. A cold, harsh winter, with northers howling through exposed houses,
caused widespread sickness; a dry spring demoralized those who worked
industriously in the fields. Some men turned to cutting wood to sell
in Dallas; others shot rabbits for a few cents apiece; still others hunted
them merely for sport. The more industrious men also supplied Dallas's
eating places with venison and homemade mustang grape wine. But
it was not enough, and the colony of upwards of three hundred folk
melted away. Some people moved into Dallas, others returned to France.
Once again Texas reality—the frontier as leveler—caught up with the
imagination and aspirations of its would-be settlers.[35]

There was a success, however, and it was called Castroville—"a French
town with a German flavor growing out of Texas soil." Castroville was
the brainchild of French financier and Texas ally Henri Castro (1786–
1865), whom President Sam Houston appointed consul general for Texas
in Paris. Castro founded his successful colony on a land grant in eastern
Medina County, about twenty-five miles west of San Antonio. Six hundred families, whom Castro recruited mostly from the French border-
land with Germany, Alsace-Lorraine, were to settle the grant. In September, 1844, Castro arrived with thirty-five colonists whom he had
selected from artisans and practical-minded folk, and during the first
year more than two thousand more arrived. Indian attacks, drought,
and cholera beset the colony, but it survived and prospered, due in large
part to Castro's zeal, competence, and industry.[36]

34. Ermance V. Rejebian, "La Réunion: The French Colony in Dallas County,"
Southwestern Historical Quarterly 43 (1940): 472–78.
35. Fischer, *Marxists,* pp. 146–53; and Ernestine P. Sewell, "La Reunion," in *The Folklore of Texan Cultures,* ed. Francis E. Abernethy, pp. 51–58.
36. Julia Nott Waugh, *Castro-Ville and Henri Castro, Empresario.*

Unduly optimistic foreign views never squarred with reality in Texas, and that fact stirred Maillard, Hooton, and others to denounce those who encouraged people to emigrate. Such advice to move to a distant, unknown, wild land was a death sentence, they argued, especially for people who were ill-suited to frontier challenges. On the other extreme, promoters and idealists alike focused on the romance of the West — Texas was a place where man could be tested and become a free individual, capable of initiative and independence. French utopians held on to these lofty ideals about the perfectibility of human nature, social equality, and self-sacrifice.

Practical-minded folk read between the lines. The information getting back to them in Europe suggested that opportunities existed for bettering their lives. Texas was a romantic setting to many German immigrants, but they also appreciated that conditions would be taxing and that they should fit themselves out for the journey. Handbooks for would-be settlers supplied instructions about what to carry: seeds, tools, clothing, even foodstuffs. Strategies for making the move, in which months, and which ports to leave from or arrive in were noted and circulated. Some immigrants looked at the region through literally jaundiced eyes. Others had been duped by overzealous promoters and were sure that preconceived images would indeed square with conditions. Most were probably less sanguine. They found descriptions of the geography and scenery attractive and appealing and their own home or national circumstances difficult and depressing enough to make them decide to move. They were prepared to accommodate themselves to a reality that they expected to be less than what they had imagined in various ways and degrees. Also, some were lucky or unlucky. Whether they believed the rosy images of Texas or not, once foreign immigrants stepped ashore, the process of settling in, of establishing and repeating routines to keep body and soul together, and of making a living absorbed them. These duties generated their own sets of impressions and expectations — mostly about prospering in this new, unfamiliar, but expanding agricultural society, and about making a home in Texas.

7. Texas as Home and Place

As we have seen, images of the environment both attracted and sustained settlement. They were vital in bringing people to Texas and in helping them adapt to the land. As settlers traveled along tracks from the east, most of which converged on Nacogdoches from the Sabine River and from the Red River in the north, they stopped and visited with those who had settled earlier. Information about where to locate, how to proceed, and which paths led to San Felipe, the heart of the first official colony, was passed along by pioneer farmers and planters. People sought out Stephen F. Austin and moved about his colony, sharing in the hospitality, which, although rude and limited, came easily on the frontier. In this sense, well-established routines for encounter and familiarization served to orient American newcomers and to make them feel a part of the settlement endeavor. As their sense of attachment grew, so did the feeling that Texas was a special place and a real home.

Foreign immigrants, as we have seen, had greater difficulties because the settlement enterprise was a completely new experience for them. Drawn from the middle classes of Western Europe, many of them were surprised by a totally different set of environmental conditions and had little guidance as to what to do in such an unfamiliar country. It is useful to follow briefly the activities and routines by which various people developed that sense of becoming Texan.

Pioneer Routines

Noah Smithwick's (1808–1899) initial impressions of Texas were a disappointment. In 1827, the nineteen-year-old youth boarded a ship in New Orleans to make his fortune in what he termed this "lazy man's paradise." The contrast between bustling wharves and ship traffic in the Mississippi Delta, where the weather was "as lovely as a dream of Venice," and the welcome from cruel-looking Karankawa Indians and a handful of Spanish-speaking residents at the landing in Matagorda Bay, Texas, was a sharp one. Texas may have possessed natural fertility, but it held the merest rudiments of culture in the eyes of the young man. Smithwick, who had contracted "Texas fever" inspired by Sterling C. Robertson's encouraging remarks on a recruiting drive for colonists, disembarked as shipmates aimed weapons at the Indians. He took a dugout canoe to a log cabin upriver, recalling later that his first meal in this new garden consisted merely of "dried venison sopped in honey."[1]

"The beautiful rose color that tinged my visions of Texas while viewing it through Robertson's long-distance lens paled with each succeeding step," declared the young pioneer. He missed creature comforts among the small band of settlers whom he joined in DeWitt's Colony, where everyone "huddled together for security" against the sullen Karankawas. The community consisted of scattered crude log cabins surrounded by fields that farmers worked using only sharp sticks. Habitations were few and far between in the massive canebrakes and dark woods populated by alligators, mosquitoes, and similarly dubious creatures.[2]

Smithwick felt especially sorry for the women who had left families and friends to come to Texas. In the newly established DeWitt's Colony he noted that they had "no house to keep in order. There was no poultry, no dairy, no garden, no books, or papers . . . no schools, no churches — nothing to break the dull monotony of their lives." In those early days such essential ingredients for making a home, of fashioning space into a lived-in place, had scarcely begun to be assembled. Settlers felt beleaguered by the untouched environment. They must also have sensed what Smithwick recognized, that the alligator's nocturnal bellow "amid the gloom and solitude of the wilderness," appeared more menacing than the same animal's vocalization in the better-lit surround-

1. Noah Smithwick, *The Evolution of a State,* pp. 1, 3.
2. Ibid., p. 4.

ings of New Orleans. The uncleared character of the land fevered the imagination.[3]

Socializing helped to establish a sense of security and belonging. Fellow Americans welcomed Smithwick, sharing food and shelter with him. He remembered how these trusty folk ministered to his periodic bouts of sickness and took him into their cabins, how his spirits improved in Sterling McNeel's household, for instance, as he hunted bears and deer and learned to shoot accurately. People's generosity and consideration for each other on the frontier helped to endear Texas to this young man. They opened their hearts to him and made him feel at home.[4]

This feeling of belonging to a community sprang up in part from the rough humor and casual ways of colonists who coined nicknames for each other, using those of domestic animals, which were scarce in early years. Everyone came to wedding suppers and dances. Young Noah enjoyed such parties in San Felipe, to which he moved in 1828, but women were so scarce that most gatherings were all-male affairs. Neighborliness and camaraderie were also reinforced through hunting; in this sense, the environment helped to solidify attachment. When he lived in San Felipe, Noah teamed up with Bob Matthews to go "gunning to see who could bag the most game." He remembered that "the boys used to come to my [blacksmith] shop to get up shooting matches," each man placing a dollar in the pot. They were a kind-hearted bunch, he concluded. Some men had come to Texas because of debts or duels, but they were basically honest, given to pranks and practical jokes, banter, and a roaring good time—except Stephen F. Austin, who "never participated in these jamborees."[5]

Settlers' ethnic prejudices served to foster closeness and exclusivity. English-speaking pioneers feared and distrusted Indians and despised Mexicans, although Smithwick praised *empresario* Martín De León, founder of Victoria, for his hospitality. Anglo settlers consorted and traveled with their own sort whenever possible. Away from settlements, the prospect of becoming lost, incapacitated by accident or illness, or surprised by violent weather also made people band together.

Environmental conditions also forced people to make adjustments, underscoring the need for assistance and cooperation. Heavy rains,

3. Ibid., pp. 5, 8.
4. Ibid., p. 18.
5. Ibid., pp. 8, 25, 40, 53.

swollen creeks, extremes of heat and cold, and long distances between cabins and communities made it natural for travelers to pause at almost any habitation and to expect and usually receive a welcome. On one occasion, Smithwick grew so homesick that he set off alone on foot toward the Brazos River estuary in hopes of finding a boat sailing for New Orleans. Panic seized him as twilight approached and in the dim light under heavy timber a rambling skunk assumed the form and size of a bloodthirsty panther. His terror diminished only when the "welcome gleam" of Captain White's dwelling appeared in the distance. The contrast between the darkness and vulnerability "outside" and security and companionship "inside" helped create the sense of belonging to a community of Texans.[6]

Texans varied, of course. East of Austin Colony, in the "Redlands," to which Smithwick was banished in 1831 for assisting a friend under criminal indictment, were squatters — a rougher and in many ways a ruthless bunch. Some worked as counterfeiters, horse thieves, land sharks, or bandits. Smithwick treated them all warily. One of his contemporaries, William P. Zuber, disliked Redlanders, as did Mexican authorities, who despised their profanity and outlaw ways. But Zuber's stay among them as a young boy lasted only six months before he moved with his parents into Austin's jurisdiction.

Georgia-born Zuber recalled that conditions in early Texas were very primitive. No more than forty people lived in the irregular rows of cabins in Harrisburg on the west bank of Buffalo Bayou in 1831, when yellow fever struck the community and carried off many, especially visitors. In a four-year span, young Zuber moved at least five times, finally making a home in two ramshackle sod huts in an abandoned Indian village in Grimes County. The young lad remembered just how isolated his family was. The nearest neighbors were always several miles away and a physician fifty or sixty. Markets for cotton and mills for corn were scarce, too, so that people subsisted largely on what they grew. The Zuber family bartered corn and vegetables for deerskins with friendly Indians, and once every two weeks or so William's father sent him to a gristmill, where he met up with boys of his own age, stayed overnight, and returned. This practice allowed him to make contacts, solidify friendships, and stay in touch with the wider community.[7]

Zuber showed a predilection for learning. On Sundays he retreated

6. Ibid., pp. 15–16.
7. Ibid., pp. 60–70; and William P. Zuber, *My Eighty Years in Texas*, pp. 29–36.

to a thicket near his cabin to read books so as not to be caught "Sabbath-breaking." At night, he waited until his parents had gone to bed, then added handfuls of brush to the fire for light and continued his reading. The simple one-room cabin was the cradle for his intellectual development. He invented a lamp—a saucer filled with the oil of raccoons that he had hunted with his dog, Patch, and a cotton wick set on a metal button to carry the flame. After 1834, when his father purchased some cattle, he used star candles made from beef tallow, which burned for a longer time. By this secretive method of home study, the teenager began to develop his intellectual curiosity and later boarded for six months with a teacher who opened a school about five miles from his home.[8]

One senses from Zuber's recollections how much he prized that youthful learning experience. The family cabin became the center for both bodily sustenance and mental nurture. Waiting up late until his parents had ceased shouting at each other (his father was deaf), then huddling next to a crackling fire to squint at the few available books whetted his desire to "escape being an ignorant and worthless animal." Mail was a hit-or-miss matter and travelers from the United States, another "source of mental improvement," were welcomed for their news of the outside world. Zuber reveals how person-to-person contacts with immigrants who were prospecting for future homes supplied residents with information that pierced the veil of isolation on the frontier.[9]

Women's Experiences

Isolation affected women especially. Smithwick sympathized with the dour struggle that women faced in early Texas. A number of commentators have agreed with him, arguing that middle-class wives and mothers found it well-nigh impossible to achieve the ideals of the "womanly woman," which southern heritage extolled in the mid-nineteenth century. The image of a passive, childlike, unreflective woman conflicted with the demands and exigencies of wilderness living. First-generation women in particular, argues researcher Ann Malone, felt themselves ill-equipped for tasks that required heavy labor and industry. Moreover,

8. Zuber, *My Eighty Years,* pp. 38–40.
9. Ibid., pp. 38–39.

they existed in a patriarchal society without the buffers of religion and a network of close kin to ease their sense of domination by men who busied themselves with making a living.[10]

Letters to friends and relatives convey homesickness, isolation, and alienation on the part of many American immigrant women who were literally uprooted from previous routines and traditions and were intimidated by their new, more ambiguous situation as helpmates in cabins on the frontier. Malone shows us how health grew into a constant anxiety—women worried constantly about children's sickness, about surviving childbirth, and about the likelihood of having to defend their homes from marauding Indians. Many middle-class women grew more and more despondent and fretful and longed to move back to communities or return to relatives and a familiar life. The loneliness they experienced from being so distant geographically from kith, kin, and other neighbors, and being so few in number and much less mobile than their husbands, elevated homemaking to a heroic occupation.[11]

Yet, in some instances their very stoicism saved them. Roles obligated them to be the harbingers of culture and gentility in raw environments, and some women became noted for their adaptability and creativity in making do in early Texas. In the 1830s, 1840s, and 1850s, they planted gardens, tended flowers, made beautiful quilts or beadwork, and superior homespun garments. In these situations the yeoman-type woman was both hardened and strengthened. Malone offers a newspaper account of one such woman on the occasion of her 110th birthday: "Mrs. Roberts is a character of Old Texas: a typical woman who shared the early hardships with her mate, never asking questions, not giving advice, but taking things as time handed them out. She never learned to read and write, and declares that she has taken up more than her allotted time here."[12] It is doubtful that this woman was "typical." The frontier dealt hard blows that required more than passive acquiescence. The lady must have questioned and come to terms with situations or events to demonstrate the resilience that allowed her to survive. She must have proffered advice to daughters or to other women. Such a woman passed on the values and ways of her antecedents. She was the line of continuity between the generations.

Mary Rabb was neither stoic nor especially heroic by pioneer stan-

10. Ann P. Malone, *Women on the Texas Frontier,* pp. 14–16.
11. Ibid., p. 17.
12. Ibid., p. 23.

dards, although she qualified as a Texas heroine in the context of contemporary norms and expectations. Rabb, in the company of husband, family, and friends, moved from Arkansas to an area near present-day La Grange in 1823. She remembered little about the six-week trek, except that most of their dozen or so cattle died and that she feasted on wild grapes and honey extracted from a bee tree. Her powers of adaptability and resilience show through, however, as she recounts how the family moved numerous times in those early years, often in response to the presence of Indians, whom she feared.

Rabb picked and spun cotton, made clothes, tended stock (a milk cow, some hogs, chickens, and dogs), raised two children, and lived a solitary existence for weeks on end when her husband was away planting a corn crop. She made camp with her family on a sandbank in the middle of the Brazos River, worrying about alligators and the possibility of flood, in order to catch the breeze that would keep mosquitoes at bay. She lived a full, unusually mobile life on the frontier as her companions opened the land for agriculture. She dealt with routines and challenges of daily existence without affectation or complaint.[13]

Women's roles changed according to status. Foreign-born women who accompanied husbands to Texas adjusted more readily to new circumstances, even to the extent of working in the fields beside their menfolk, something Rabb did not do. Englishwoman Amelia Barr, for example, came with her Scottish husband, Robert, and two baby daughters from earlier homes in Chicago and Memphis. She adjusted well to Texas conditions, demonstrating curiosity about the new land and its people. Barr delighted in the appearance of Galveston—"A city in a garden"—but traveled on to Harrisburg because of an outbreak of yellow fever in the port. Harrisburg, too, was bedeviled by sickness, so the Barr family set out almost immediately for Austin, their final destination. Most of the journey was by horse-drawn coach and included a night in Bastrop, where the "many signs of drawing near to civilization" included a hotel, comfortable rooms, and good food consisting of beef and venison in place of monotonous bacon, and both corn and squash.

The owner of the hotel was a widow and visited with Amelia. "I'm kind of lonesome," she murmured, asking to hold one of Barr's little girls. She had lost her husband, Jake, who "took ill and died suddent one night, just after Mollie [her surviving daughter] came home. I miss Jake whiles, though he left me well-to-do, and a full sorrow is easier

13. Mary C. Rabb, *Travels and Adventures in Texas in the 1820's*, pp. 1–2, 8, 10.

borne than an empty one," she sighed. Amelia Barr's hostess, looking down at the little girl sleeping in her arms, added that "babies are hard to raise in Texas . . . you can never call your child your own in Texas, until it has passed its second year." She had herself lost five out of seven children.[14]

That night the woman invited Amelia into her parlor, away from stony-faced men gambling at cards. It was furnished with a handsome piano, upholstered chairs, pictures, and crocheted lace fashioned by the woman's only living daughter, Mollie. Amelia "felt a great respect for the girl [Mollie] who had lifted herself so far above her surroundings." Next morning, she ushered herself and her children into the coach for the final stage to Austin: "we left the hospitable lady with many kind words and wishes. At last she kissed the children, and I, remembering my own mother, kissed her; for about a good woman, who had taken the sacrament of maternity, there is the odor and sense of sacrifice. We may touch her lips, and do her honor, and be sure that we are honoring ourselves in the homely rite."[15] Amelia left on the final leg to Austin, which she called "Arcadia," leaving behind a new friend who was rich in material goods, but starving for the companionship of other women who could supply both sympathy and understanding about domestic details and matters of the heart.

Companionship abounded in socially sophisticated Austin in the mid-1850s. The Barr family took a four-room, two-story wooden house, the need for paint, plaster, and general refurbishment of which Amelia dismissed as "picturesque irregularities." More significantly, she was most happy when she "stood once more on my own hearth." She selected furniture, including a four-poster bed like ones found in English farmhouses, and set to cleaning. After three weeks she was satisfied with her "pretty home," having "plenty of fine bedding, and table damask, china and plates, some favorable books, and bits of bric-a-brac, a few pictures and rugs, and a good deal of Berlin wool work, and fancy needlework."[16]

Well-to-do white women like herself, whose husbands worked for the state government or were successful in Austin businesses, led socially exclusive lives in the capital city. "Women are never democratic," she opined. Having servants made it possible for these Austin women to enjoy

---

14. Amelia Barr, *All the Days of My Life,* pp. 178, 181, 185, 186–87.
15. Ibid., p. 189.
16. Ibid., pp. 195, 204–205.

an endless tucking of fine muslin, and inserting lace in the same. Very little but white swiss or mull was worn, and morning and evening dresses were known by the amount of tucking and lace which adorned them. Some of the women chewed snuff without cessation, and such women neither "tucked," nor "inserted." They simply rocked to-and-fro, and put in a word occasionally. It must be remembered that the majority of women who "dipped" had likely formed the habit, when it was their only physical tranquilizer, through days and nights of terror, and pain, and watchfulness; and that the habit once formed is difficult to break, even if they desired to break it, which was not a common attitude.[17]

The customary gathering routine was to send word to a lady that several friends intended to visit the following morning. From 9:00 A.M. to 4:00 P.M., ladies gathered to talk with one another. They quickly changed into loose garments and slippers, "took out their tucking, and palm leaf fans, and subsided into rocking-chairs," observed Mrs. Barr, noting that "they could all talk well." Lunch consisted of broiled quail breasts and potpie of wild turkey or venison washed down with strong coffee. In the later afternoon, they changed back into street clothes, gathered their handiwork, and went home to await their menfolk, who were excluded, but much talked about, from such situations.[18]

These houses were centers for daily relaxation and informality and filled the role that theaters, libraries, and conservatories played in later years. Such intimate gatherings were strictly segregated by status and gender and men were wary of them. Robert Barr used to ask Amelia about the subject of their conversation, but she always dodged his queries. He appears to have resigned himself to or accepted such gatherings. His wife certainly drew emotional sustenance from them while Robert was establishing himself as an accountant for the state's Treasury Department.

Amelia Barr did not know how widespread this practice of visiting was in rural places, but she reckoned that resourcefulness among Texas womanhood would bring them together. She regarded them as brave and competent in household duties, even in the management of their ranches when their husbands were absent. "They were then nearly without exception fine riders and crack shots, and quite able . . . to keep such faithful guard over their families and household."[19]

17. Ibid., pp. 206–207.
18. Ibid., pp. 207–208.
19. Ibid., p. 211.

Amelia Barr exaggerated such skills, but not the courage or resilience needed for living in Texas a generation or more after Noah Smithwick expressed his sympathy for women. Austin was naturally positioned on the edge of the cattle- and sheep-raising region where ranching culture thrived after the Civil War. There, a woman had to be able to ride a horse and handle a gun to protect herself and deal with varmints and critters that raided livestock.

Kate Rogers, "daughter of the Big Bend," was one of Barr's "fine riders and crack shots." She was born in 1879, twelve years after Amelia Barr had left Texas forever after the tragic deaths of her husband and three sons. Rogers's father was an avid hunter who "was never without hound dogs till the day he died." He hunted panthers in the Chisos Mountains, part of today's Big Bend National Park, then purchased a ranch in the Nine-Point Mountains. "I had been using a gun since I was ten years old . . . to kill snakes, hawks or squirrels," admitted Kate, so hunting stock-killing mountain lions and deer and javelina came naturally. In eight years spent in Big Bend, Kate Rogers took part in "lots of panther chases. . . . I have got up at 2 or 3 o'clock in the morning many a time and saddled my horse and started out alone on a hunt with the dogs. I always carried a little .39 pistol for my protection," she recalled. She turned her trophies into moccasins, gloves, or rugs in the winter months. Expert with both a gun and a rope, this Calamity Jane character grew into a trusted ranch hand. Rogers felt completely at home in the Chihuahuan desert landscape beyond the Pecos River. Many years after she had moved away from the harsh environment, Rogers observed, "You feel the BIGNESS of the land where you are only a human being and I know that the years my eyes looked on the beauty I saw everywhere, were years added to my life."[20]

Like others born on the Texas frontier, Kate Rogers adjusted to conditions, accepting without murmur the uncertainties that living in isolation presented. Like Mary Rabb, she took conditions in her stride. In her case, it was tending livestock rather than grain and cotton crops that made up the work in her life. Neither woman was especially unusual. Although Amelia Barr's daily life was more comfortable than Rogers's, her commitment had to be equally strong. She had left her home in England for a distant land, making a sharp break with family and friends. She offers a vignette of daily life among Austin's middle-class at mid-

20. Florence Fenley, "Mrs. Kate Rogers," in *Oldtimers of Southwest Texas*, pp. 74–78.

century. The human concerns have not changed; only the particulars and current opportunities for personal expression differ substantially from her much more circumscribed existence.

Foreigners Find a Home

Foreigners of both sexes steeled themselves to make a major break with the past to adjust to conditions as they found them. Still they encountered considerable difficulty in making their preconceived images square with reality. One of them, Emanuel Domenech, a French seminarian ordained in Texas, enjoyed the protection, such as it was, of the Catholic church.

Responding to Bishop John M. Odin's visit to Lyons, France, in the late 1840s to appeal for missionaries, young Father Domenech immigrated to Texas. He enjoyed the flowers, bluebirds, and different insects that he happened upon along the road to Castroville, his first parish. But no one attended his first mass in the run-down church, and his ignorance of German, which most of his flock spoke, made communication difficult. His initial home was a wood, stone, and brick structure, built by two former priests who had died. It consisted of two rooms separated by a dogtrot. Fissures in the walls allowed free access to insects and rodents. Increasingly despondent, Domenech established himself in one of the rooms but found the ants on the bare earth floor so bothersome that he took to sleeping in a hammock. He felt so bewildered and lost that he "fell into mortal ennui before the end of a fortnight."

The appearance of the community did nothing to bolster his spirits. Castroville was a mere collection of huts overgrown with weeds concealing abundant wildlife, including snakes, with which he had several encounters. He mentioned one dead rattler measuring a preposterous seventeen feet, eight inches. Food was his constant preoccupation. He lived off a sparse vegetable patch, dried venison, and handouts from parishioners. He feasted on alligators, cooked snakes, and even ate domestic cats.[21]

Domenech's spirits revived after a fellow priest joined him and when

21. Emanuel H. Dieudonne Domenech, *Missionary Adventures in Texas*, pp. 44, 47, 51, 52.

his clerical duties began to produce a favorable response from Catholics in the community. Familiarity and perhaps boredom with his immediate surroundings increased his boldness and led to an excursion to Dhanis, some thirty-five miles west of Castroville. He passed a cold night in the chaparral, his draft animals strayed, and gloomy weather depressed him again. Years later he recalled how easy it was to lose one's way in the thick vegetation, mentioning that searchers had found the bleached skeletons of colonists who had also been lost and exposed to Indian attack in the seemingly endless brush country.

As time passed, however, the foreign priest's confidence grew and he found pleasure in parish duties. Paradoxically, an epidemic of cholera turned his ministry into a rewarding one, although he was left dog tired by the constant summonses to treat and comfort the afflicted and administer the last rites to moribund parishioners.[22]

The word *home* proved a mockery to some settlers, notably a group of German immigrants who came in under the auspices of the Adelsverein in the mid-1840s. More than seven thousand of them landed in Texas, and for many it was a "journey of death." Incompetent officials, logistical difficulties, and mismanagement compounded problems of moving the newcomers from Indianola to New Braunfels.

The new home in Texas was glimpsed through a thickening veil of despondency, sickness, and hardship. The primitive landing at Indianola was open to wind and rain; it had inadequate water, fuelwood, and sanitation. People began to die. Those who ventured on the laborious journey inland suffered dysentery and other maladies in the "comfortless prairie, glowing with the heat of the sun. . . . Along the road lay human bones, together with beds, tools, chests, and trunks," noted a historian, as desperate Germans abandoned utensils and cherished possessions. Those who had almost reached New Braunfels were cut off by the swollen Comal River and suffered terribly in crude shelters along its banks. Schoolteacher Hermann Seele visited with his countrymen and was shocked to see their helplessness. He spoke with a sick man whose

cheeks burned with a dull red; his eyes glittered with uncommon brightness. He wanted to let me know that he had no more pain—that he now felt better, and soon would be in a position to return with his wife and children to his beloved homeland. . . . And when the sun rose next morning, the sick man had calmly gone to rest. We dug his grave in the field, laid him gently down, and prayed a silent *Vater unser* for him and his family. Years passed

22. Ibid., pp. 94–95, 98–99.

away; the dead man rested in the grave with others whom we buried there. The green grass had long covered it when the railroad came to New Braunfels. There the railroad workers came upon a few bones preserved in the sandy soil, and scraped them in again. Now the train rolls over the place in haste.[23]

Suffering was familiar to Father Domenech, yet he was able to draw courage and strength from administering the faith to fellow humans. In New Braunfels, schoolteacher Seele regarded the dying man's plight and suffering as a terrible waste. No one remembered his name; the train rumbled over his bones. Yet this tragedy, repeated time and again, drew out the humanity of settlers who gave of themselves to help their fellows.

There is a peculiarly geographical aspect to this rhythm of life and death, a sense of "presence" that author A. C. Greene has perceptively noted in the land around his boyhood home of Abilene, Texas. "When you come upon some spot where man was and is no more," Greene writes, "the ground speaks." He was thinking in particular of a field south of Albany in Shackelford County, where the faintest traces of saltwork remain. In the incident of the dying man outside New Braunfels, the ground speaks to that bond of identity forged by the sacrifice of the immigrant and his kinfolk. His death served to cement the sense of belonging and self-consciousness among the steadfast German Texans, giving to their settlements a special stamp of home and dwelling that endures to this day.[24]

The House and Natural Place

Home was fashioned by willpower and the experiences of pioneers and settlers. Ideally, it offered both refuge and prospect. In physical terms, the cabin, house, or plantation defined space by circumscribing it and by stamping it with that unique character formed from the objects and events that it bounded. In this way, place emerges as a humanly ordered space centered around a dwelling that offers protection and sustenance. The personal sense of well-being fostered by the refuge and prospect defines the individual's identity and attachment to his or her home place.

23. Samuel W. Geiser, *Naturalists of the Frontier,* pp. 112–13.
24. A. C. Greene, *A Personal Country,* p. 263.

Home symbolizes the commitment of lifeblood and industry on the part of individuals who have given energy and resources to family and community. People like author William A. Owens are saddened to return to their childhood farms and find that the buildings have rotted away, the well has caved in, and only a chinaberry tree or some other ornamental plant or two survives. But the farmstead, like the fields and towns in the larger environment around it, has given a certain stamp to the region. Novelist Greene says that "every man has a village in his heart, whether he comes from abounding Manhattan or the prairies of West Texas." The old community is a reference point in life's decisions, so that in returning to Charity in East Texas, as William Goyen does in his novel *The House of Breath*, the house, community, and landscape reconvene the dialogue that he initiated as a child. The same patterns of thought, routines of movement, and images come flooding back. The home place, therefore, retains its bonds even though many of the buildings may have disappeared or been turned to new purposes.[25]

The home place was especially significant on a personal level because of the special events and human personalities that it nurtured. Goyen likens his house, now in ruin, to a person's breath. The site, with its weathered, ramshackle features, expresses intense emotional bonds. They are a reliquary, holding memories of earlier days and of the characters of the many kin who grew up within their confines, left, and perhaps returned to die, languishing behind faded shutters, calling out in turn for the loved ones who had played and worked within the younger house. But like breath, memories are spent and discarded and lost from consciousness; yet, like breath, they remain part of humanity's birth and death, love and hate — an ever-recurring pattern of inhalation into the womb and wellspring of our being.

As such, the house as a home provides the focus for human interest and concern, for yearly and seasonal activities of work and play, and for distant and near travel. As Texas grew more and more familiar to the countless travelers and settlers passing along its routes, the man-altered spaces, the cabins and cleared lands between settlements, replaced the natural character of the wilderness. The vast untrammeled wildland was scaled down to human order and addressed in human terms. This brings us back to the ideas of wilderness and garden, and to the meanings these held for people in early Texas.

25. Ibid., p. 112; William A. Owens, *A Season of Weathering*, p. 193; and William Goyen, *The House of Breath*, pp. 6–7, 46–47, passim.

Symbolic Landscapes

The wilderness and garden are symbolic landscapes; that is, they are landscapes that store information about human values. Symbolic landscapes, like other symbols, represent a kind of shorthand that people use to convey information. The wilderness stands for an unaltered landscape in which the forces of nature rather than of man dominate. By contrast, the garden symbolizes transformed space in which settlement and industry are conspicuous, that is, where human activities express themselves in conventional forms by exploiting a fertile resource base. In the first instance, people frequently refer to the symbol of wilderness to set themselves apart, in opposition to nature, although, as we have seen, many pioneers discovered methods of coping with long distances and isolation and environmental constraints. In the latter instance, the garden stood for a rich, beneficent environment in which settlers could plan a bright future.

On a deeper level, the two symbolic landscapes are contrasted by being in turn profane and sacred. The wilderness environment is intrinsically profane in the Anglo-European and Christian mind: it is the end product of blind and irrational natural forces stretching back into a pagan, primitive epoch. Indeed, the Indian may have viewed those pristine and unsullied environments — the ones that Austin described — with reverence and with a sense of belonging to them, of being "inside." All the more reason, therefore, why pioneers who were intent on rendering order out of chaos, on "chastising" the Indians and making the wilderness habitable, detested the intrinsic disorder and sought to turn the wilderness into the garden, into sacred space.

Their religious convictions confirmed their sense of moral rectitude and justified taking and holding land, just as ranchers claimed piously that they were saving rangelands from decay. One propagandist claimed that his mission was to precede the agriculturalist: "It was his to establish and maintain, with profit to the state, a valuable industry. He represented as it were, an era—an epoch—a step in social progress."[26]

The wilderness is transformed into the garden by human presence, which selects what it needs from the environment and banishes what is harmful. Some observers concentrated on the former, emphasizing the functional uses of natural Texas. For them, the garden was already

26. Goyen, *House of Breath*, p. 60.

present, requiring only appropriate tilling and exploitation to tap its enormous fertility.

The image of the garden was an especially effective promotional device and a rationalization for human presence. It was also the symbol of a secure land, of a man-modified or cultural landscape where obstacles had been removed or suppressed. It represented the continued "Europeanization" of the New World, extending this process from neighboring southern states.

The garden was also sacred space because it represented man's creativity and industry in a historic time frame and on a human, even personal, scale. One geographer has referred to cultural landscapes as archives in that they record the narrative of human occupation. As artifacts of group solidarity and livelihood, they show a sharing of human experiences. They also demonstrate how people have come into conflict with nature and aboriginal cultures, and the specific ways in which such conflicts have been resolved.

Natural Place

Characteristics of the environment in and for itself engaged people's attention. There was in this sense a *natural* place in Texas that could become a *natural* home. It was a combination of soils, relief, and vegetation that shifted markedly as one passed from east to west. Toward the Sabine River existed a vegetation zone consisting of a closely spaced, dark overstory of tall pines. These conifers plus hickory, oaks, and other subhumid woody species from the South presented a clutter of small habitats. The enveloping screen of vegetation and low sand or gravel ridges between a network of creeks and rivers dominated the landscape, shutting in its few human denizens and blocking out the sky. This belt of shadowing pines and hardwoods, the proverbial untouched wilderness, presented closed and darkened space, which human enterprise opened up only by clearing and settling.

On the other extreme, West Texas was a landscape open to a distant, low horizon and dominated by the daily and seasonal rhythms of the sky—a "cosmic" environment. Endless changes in cloud formations affected the quality of light above a monotonous ground. Many settlers saw this broad, flatland expanse as a permanent, timeless place.

Some of them felt overpowered by the limitless horizon, recognizing their own smallness and sensing their limitations; they faced the absolute. "The loneliness of the high sky makes men see God. But he is seen in the fiery sunlight," comments native West Texan Green, who is reminded in the dry desert country and its low blue hills of "the Biblical lands." Kate Rogers saw beauty in the bigness of the land.[27]

People experienced both kinds of forest and plains wilderness. But they also knew a "middle ground" in which earth and sky elements seemed to balance each other. This was the natural garden, and it existed in the rolling or undulating prairies of the central zone, north of the coastal plain, east of the Balcones Escarpment, and west of the Trinity River. It was a perfect or "classical landscape," and Stephen F. Austin recognized it immediately. He located his land grant between the Brazos and Colorado rivers in the heart of this rolling zone and extended it out onto the coastal plain. Middle Texas was neither impenetrable woodland nor monotonous open desert; it was a "parkland" of pines, oaks, and other useful trees, and possessed excellent openings and prairies for livestock and tillage. Earth and sky elements seemed to complement each other so that the rolling horizon and embracing sky vault made the character of this region essentially pleasing and human in scale. The trees, openings, and gentle hills formed a patchwork of distinct individual places that settlers and travelers quickly took to heart. Holley loved this zone; German immigrants made it their home; promoters eulogized it; utopians planned for the millennium there. In the classical sense, then, Central Texas was a natural home for Anglo and European peoples, as it incorporated the ideal images of Western cultural landscapes.[28]

Another element in the natural place of Texas to which early settlers responded was direction. As on the American frontier in general, uncharted and unappropriated lands lay in the west. But "west" in Texas also meant Mexico and the Hispanic culture represented by San Antonio. West spelled conflict, conflict with a prior colonial power that stood in the way of "Americanization," as Austin termed his vision of manifest destiny, conflict also with American Indians who inhabited the unsecured western range lands, living off wild bison and periodi-

27. Greene, *A Personal Country*, pp. 128, 127.
28. See Christian Norberg-Schulz, *Genius Loci: Towards a Phenomenology of Architecture*, for a discussion of cosmic and classical landscapes.

cally sweeping in from the plateau and plains to harass settlers and steal livestock. West, therefore, pointed toward insecurity, but also to unclaimed, fertile, free, and abundant land. As an expression of order in the natural landscape, the idea of moving west proved critical in the pull and push of the Texas frontier.

Texas as a natural place for human activities also included marked seasonal rhythms, when different moisture and temperature regimes took over the land and affected life's patterns. Seasonal contrasts were not as marked as in northern regions, but cold Arctic winds swept down from the plains, and in summer a searing sun burned up the plateau and desert uplands.

Seasons occurred differently in the three divisions. In the open, flat landscapes of the High Plains and Gulf Coast prairies, rain, snow, and cold spells often made movement difficult. Travelers and other people unfamiliar with these monotonous regions became disoriented when rough tracks and stone markers disappeared under snow or mud and low visibility blotted out distant landmarks. The immense stands of ten- or fifteen-foot-high cane along the lower reaches of the Brazos River were notorious impediments to movement, just as the "flag" marshes of tall reeds around Beaumont crazed waterfowl hunters who got lost in them in the 1880s. Similarly, the expanse of brush country in South Texas was known for its impenetrability, especially during rainy or overcast conditions. French priest Emanuel Domenech noted how a colleague disappeared into the thick chaparral and was never seen again.

Someone has observed that the mesquite tree, thorny, resilient, and rough coated, is a fitting symbol for both South and West Texas. The wind, too, is an essential ingredient in natural place. In West Texas it is always there, carrying the tilt and swing of vultures and the cranes' "scrawling trail of loud calligraphy on vacant sky." The wind forces people to adjust with automatic gestures, leaning into it, holding hats, brushing away grit; it adds to the loneliness already present. In Dorothy Scarborough's novel *The Wind*, the heroine, a newcomer to West Texas, is finally driven insane by the incessant blowing.[29]

Summer conditions were just as difficult. Insect pests such as chiggers, flies, and even locusts bothered travelers on the sweltering plains.

29. Greene, *A Personal Country*, pp. 151–52; Owens, *A Season of Weathering*, pp. 27–29; Dorothy Scarborough, *The Wind*; and William Barney, "The Cranes at Muleshoe," in *The Killdeer Crying*, p. 74.

Toward the coast, miasma or wind-borne vapors from swamps were believed to bring on agues and fevers. Sea breezes helped cool inhabitants, but mosquitoes proved ferocious. One old-timer remembered being unable to determine the color of a colt because these blood-sucking insects packed themselves so tightly over its hide.

The central or middle zone of Texas, by contrast, enjoyed the mildest and best mix of seasons. The bursting forth of flora and fauna in spring, especially the brilliantly colored wild flowers, drew universal praise. People were invigorated year round by a warm sun, bright light, and blue skies. The clarity and intensity of light in Texas caused by its low latitude made the environment sparkling and fresh.

Early Texans responded to the environment in a variety of ways. We have seen that some folk focused on the bucolic and pastoral qualities of the landscape; others literally created a home away from home by discovering visual similarities with European landscapes; and others devoted themselves to pleasurable hunting and exploration. All these helped to develop a sense of attachment and belonging.

Images of natural Texas as well as humanly altered Texas attracted and sustained settlers. They still do. In large part these essentially rural ideas have lost ground to contemporary interest in urban space: in metroplexes, golden triangles, and megalopolises, life is displayed in the holy garb of mobility, immediate gratification, and distraction. Time is money and so is space when reduced to a commodity for real estate speculation and land development, as many did in promoting the Garden. But there is a need for place.

A number of literary people remind us how Texans organized their space. William A. Owens's recollections of his childhood in Pin Hook, in northeast Lamar County, show the struggle that his widowed mother endured in raising five children on not-so-fertile land. His twentieth-century experiences are three generations or more removed from Smithwick's and Zuber's time, but conditions are similar in several respects. Pin Hook was an isolated community in a lonely land tortured by extreme weather, often stinting in its crop yields. Owens had his belly filled with soil beginning when his mother tethered him to prevent him from crawling off into the woods with the scorpions and snakes while she labored in the cotton fields. He learned quickly that "sights and smells go with the seasons." Similarly, Elmer Kelton's central character, Charles Flagg, felt his drought-stricken Rio Concho home in West Texas to be "an ageless land where the past was still a living thing and old voices still whispered, where the freshness of the pioneer time had not all faded."[30]

Larry McMurtry has rejected this special concern for personal space, for home and attachment to land as place, as unduly pastoral and nostalgic. He looks to contemporary metropolitan living for the stimulus to imagination and creativity. Others, too, including Owens, recognize with Goyen that "there seemed something more magnificent" than home, and that is loneliness. Something drew Goyen and Owens and other Texas authors away from the "quiet and dying old life." Yet they returned because they needed to recall and reconnect. In Greene's words, he returned to search for "a boy and a man in a place, and part of that place in them." It was a personal return to write about events and places of emotional value, to ask if we are "not gifted from the soil from whence we sprang, seeded by the people, and watered by the times."[31]

Their words contrast with McMurtry's because these writers recognize in themselves the desire to get away from home to gain the perspective from which to articulate explicitly their relationship to it. Images of places and the events connected with them are the base for the sense of continuity that each one of us needs. We remember our childhood environments. They are the benchmark against which we measure our intellectual and spiritual growth; they are the anvils upon which our values and attitudes toward life are forged. But memories of such places should not be steeped in a nostalgia that attempts only to recall and refabricate the superficial form (the pioneer's log cabin, for instance) without the substance. The substance is the authentic relationship between humans and the world that must be fashioned by each individual; it cannot be borrowed from the past. It is that substance that is the wellspring for group and regional identities; it shapes vocabularies, patterns of communication, and behavior.

30. William A. Owens, *This Stubborn Soil: A Frontier Boyhood,* p. 13; and Elmer Kelton, *The Time It Never Rained,* p. 9.

31. Larry McMurtry, "Ever a Bridegroom: Reflections on the Failure of Texas Literature," *Texas Observer* (October 23, 1981): 1, 8–19; Goyen, *House of Breath,* p. 109; and Greene, *A Personal Country,* pp. 1–2.

8. Conclusion

"Wilderness" and "Garden" are two important operative images in the nineteenth-century settlement of Texas. Both concepts served to encapsulate general yet detached or distant views of the land, suggesting implicitly what attitudes newcomers should adopt and how they should set about dealing with the environment. The wilderness image contrasted human needs with what the land had to offer. It suggested that human activities should be aimed at the transformation and control of the land. Wilderness had to be forced to accommodate settlement through dedicated work. This was Austin's vision—and why he wished to recruit tough, resilient pioneers who would hew forests, pull out tree stumps, burn canebrakes, and plant crops, thereby improving the land and demonstrating human skill, ingenuity, and the march of civilization. The land was not simply the stage on which civilization expressed itself; it struck back, fighting against the bridle and bit like an unbroken mustang.

This view pitting man against the environment fitted the stereotype of a Texan who took crop failure or flood in stride, became accustomed to weather vagaries, and adjusted well to a strange, thinly populated region. Austin managed rather than welcomed such leatherstocking characters. He really wanted the "better sort" of Texans, especially the monied class of Southern planters, who, because of their education and heightened social sense, would be prepared to make the same sacrifices as he was. The vision of Texan identity and continuity demanded self-sacrifice, and he hoped that these Americans understood the rites of passage—

the eradication of wilderness—on behalf of themselves and the collective good.

The Garden represented a Texas-to-be, a subdued wildness that obediently provided for human needs. The practice of turning back the wilderness to create the garden required time, ingenuity, and effort. Whether Texas was to be fashioned into a garden or needed only embellishments to an existing Eden, the image was of the land whose elements had responded to man's activities and were reduced thereby to a human scale. In this scenario, the environment would cooperate and respond to human enterprise, which improved on nature.

This image of Texas represented the union of the best soils, water, vegetation, fauna, and climate, especially where Austin's grant was located. The garden metaphor drew together all nature's resources, showed them off, and encouraged Texas yeomen to exploit them. The image was highly romanticized. Promoters deliberately exaggerated in picturing Texas as an Italian or Mediterranean garden. This simple, classical motif represented a rolling terrain full of light and sunshine where rural communities were surrounded by orchards and grain fields and tended livestock. Texas was a stylized Mediterranean landscape garden.

Such idyllic images also spelled out control of the land. Settlers would populate this new Mediterranean by carrying in appropriate plants and animals that afforded sustenance plus profit. The actual Hispanic components that formed the real, tangible link with the Old World Mediterranean drew attention only after the Civil War, when the tourist industry, spurred by the spread of railroads into Texas, discovered in San Antonio and its missions the actual Mediterranean heritage, which visitors regarded as a museum exhibit.

Settlement involves working within a framework of existing images. The settler proceeds to build a sense of home and becomes attached to a new world through the episodes and routines that happen there. He or she may change, clarify, or discard generally accepted images in the context of day-to-day routines. The terms "wilderness" and "garden" provided a structure for activity and a boundary for Texas space in the manner of a landscape painter who gathers together the elements, perspective, and frame to compose the picture. The painter projects his or her values into the landscape in the very act of assessing it. In a similar manner, Austin's frequent reference to wilderness established a framework for understanding the land, but in a specific and conventional way, as godless and uncivilized terrain requiring subjugation and transformation. There was no conscious intention to accept or understand the land for itself. The garden image may have made the land appear to be more tractable, but it was an environment calling for human enterprise, not acceptance, to transform natural conditions into an appropriate cultural landscape.[1]

In either case, the pioneer was forced to make adjustments to survive and prosper. Family or friends had to clear away vegetation, plant a crop, hunt, cook, care for children — grounding themselves in the actual experience of living on the land. This experience went beyond images and may or may not have squared with them. Ordinary folk like Rabb, Zuber, Nicholls, and Kuykendall experienced what Texas had to give and take, so that, rather than the unidimensional and threatening image of wilderness as a symbol for control, or as benchmark against which to measure civilization's progress, or a more benign one of bucolic redolence, the land became differentiated into a patchwork of distinct places. It was filled with the sounds, smells, and colors of daily and seasonal rhythms together with memories of the various families who had lived there.

Establishing a home required an understanding of nature and of how to exploit it. Settlers recognized what Texas was good for and how important it was for their family and friends to cooperate in drawing from the abundant soils, water, and wildlife. These early Texans were knowledgeable and tough. Many of them were brothers of Scots and Irish "border warriors" who had moved steadily westward from the Atlantic seaboard over the course of three or four generations. But it is too simple to think of them as a hard, humorless bunch dedicated only to work. There was much more to them than dourness. Homemaking cannot be defined exclusively in economic terms.

As Texas took on a human face in the form of settlements and cultivation, its denizens grew confident enough to enjoy the land for itself. Leisure and that sense of being established and secure in a new place meant that they could think of satisfying more than immediate, material needs. Smithwick recalled the good times in San Felipe. He loved to go hunting and remembered the banter and good-natured ribbing on such excursions. He enjoyed the rough humor, casual ways, and zest for life. One learned about the personalities of friends and colleagues, as well as about the character of the land, its geography, and about the behavior and life histories of different animals. This feeling of identity and of belonging stemmed from a fellowship that was gained

1. See Denis Cosgrove, *Social Formation and Symbolic Landscape,* pp. 20–27.

Conclusion

from hardship—from winning over the environment and meeting its challenges—and from cooperating with others to fashion a community. Many people liked the land because it was useful, but also because it was interesting, beautiful, and personally fulfilling.

Daniel Shipman, for example, remembered how the mockingbird's song welcomed him on the lonely road to Texas in 1822. The "little feathered musicians" cheered him as he camped out and accentuated the vibrant character of the spring landscape. A colony of brown pelicans near the port of Galveston interested and amused immigrants, most of whom had never seen these birds before. Scotsman David Edward admired the comical-looking waterbirds when noting the "immense flocks" of waterfowl that inhabited Galveston Bay and caused endless noise and commotion. Even Olmsted set aside his prejudices to exult over the beauty of the flower-decked prairies. Such accounts of interesting animals, plants, and attractive scenery typify many early accounts. Pleasure from the land and its inhabitants relieved the tension of being in such a strange, distant region and added a lighter side to life and the encounter with Texas.[2]

Our ability to know the world in an unconscious or taken-for-granted sense is the heart of the experience of being at home. It is that feeling of being familiar and comfortable in a place or situation. The passage of time is necessary for the experience of place. The individual develops a feeling of ease by repeated interactions with his or her world on a day-to-day basis so that at-homeness grows gradually.

Images of what Texas was supposed to be framed the settler's initial approach to the land. But as the years passed, the process of dwelling and establishing attachment concretized the image, making it specific, workable, and full. People set about reorganizing the environment, accepting naturally their roles as modifiers of the land. They drew on the complexity and availability of resources. Familiarity was founded on time spent in a location and on routines of making ends meet.

It was also appropriate to set these routines and life's "many tryels and troubbles" (as Mary Rabb stated it) in a larger context. Difficulties often served to strengthen the sense of belonging to a place, for dealing with them called for faith in oneself, in friends, and in God. Rabb wrote to her children that "God was mindful of us and blesst us and gave us his spirit and made us feel that we was his." Personal fortunes, fel-

2. Daniel Shipman, *Frontier Life: 58 Years in Texas*, pp. 19–20; David B. Edward, *The History of Texas*, p. 61; and Frederick Law Olmsted, *A Journey through Texas*, p. 233.

lowship, and belief in a divine purpose deepened the experience of home.[3]

"Dwelling" in the European sense of practicing land husbandry as a means of conserving a lifeway and incorporating into it knowledge about manures and crop or stock rotation so as not to exhaust the soil did not occur in early Texas. Such practices, notably those developed from England's farm improvements and crop experiments after the mid-1700s, were adopted only slowly in the United States and hardly at all on the frontier. In Texas, the cusotm was to move (usually westward) when crops failed and soils gave out. Unclaimed land was not at a premium, as in Europe; therefore, the idea of dwelling did not signify husbandry or land management in terms of conserving a specific portion, but the actual involvement with the transformation process itself and preparedness to move on as land wore down.

Edward Everett Dale, for example, recalled in his vivid memoir of growing up in the Cross Timbers how his father had cleared a fifty-six-acre farm by cutting his own timber and building a four-room log house, complete with a cellar, corncrib, shed, and barn. He remembered how they planted peach, apple, and plum trees, set out a grape arbor, cleared a pasture for horses, kept bees, and tended a vegetable plot. Unexpectedly, however, his father decided to move farther west. After working this land for a dozen years or so, he decided he had done all he could and was ready to do it all again.[4]

Today's urban dweller has lost that feeling of being involved with the land in the way that Dale knew. Practical and thorough understanding about the life of the seasons and of what the land was good for in its fabric of soils and vegetation has grown scarce. Because of this, the essential connections and enjoyment that settlers experienced and that we seek in periodic excursions into the countryside are dulled by the fact that we are spectators, outsiders who are unable to grasp the subtleties of the land's moods and changes.

By working with their hands, colonists took part in creation and derived immense satisfaction from understanding their rural lifeworld. We need to open ourselves up to the historical framework by which they fashioned that identity of becoming Texan. We must recognize also that the urge to identify with a place — to be at home — remains as strongly

3. Mary Crownover Rabb, *Travels and Adventures in Texas in the 1820's*, p. 14.
4. Edward Everett Dale, *The Cross Timbers: Memories of a North Texas Boyhood*, p. 167.

embedded in us as in the pioneers. By developing individual and genuine affection and appreciation for the texture of that natural life that surrounds and supports us, contemporary residents can lift themselves beyond nostalgia, boosterism, or provincialism and discover how the region called Texas is both the stage and the actor in life's continuous drama.

Bibliography

Abernethy, Francis E. *The Folklore of Texan Cultures.* Austin: Encino Press, 1974.

Adams, Ephraim D., ed. *British Diplomatic Correspondence Concerning the Republic of Texas, 1838–1846.* Austin: Texas State Historical Association, 1918[?].

"Agriculture Capacities of Western Texas." *De Bow's Review* 18 (1855): 54–55.

Allen, Elsa G. *The History of American Ornithology before Audubon.* Philadelphia: American Philosophical Society, 1951.

Allen, John Taylor. *Early Pioneer Days in Texas.* Dallas: Wilkinson, 1918.

Almonte, Juan. "Statistical Report on Texas." Edited and translated by C. E. Castañeda. *Southwestern Historical Quarterly* 28 (1925): 177–222.

Ashford, Gerald. *Spanish Texas: Yesterday and Today.* Austin: Jenkins, 1971.

Ashliman, D. L. "The Novel of Western Adventure in Nineteenth-Century Germany." *Western American Literature* 3 (1968): 133–45.

[Austin, Stephen F.]. "Journal of Stephen F. Austin on His First Trip to Texas, 1821." *Quarterly of the Texas State Historical Association* 7 (1904): 286–307.

Baker, T. Lindsay. *The First Polish Americans: Silesian Settlements in Texas.* College Station: Texas A&M University Press, 1979.

Barba, Preston A. "The American Indian in German Fiction." *German American Annals* 15 (1913): 143–74.

———. "Cooper in Germany." *German American Annals* 12 (1914): 3–60.

———. "Emigration as Reflected in German Fiction." *German American Annals* 12 (1914): 193–227.

———. *The Life and Works of Friedrich Armand Strubberg.* American Germanica, vol. 16. Philadelphia: University of Pennsylvania, 1913.

147

Barbour, Ian G., ed. *Western Man and Environmental Ethics.* Reading, Mass.: Addison-Wesley, 1973.

Barker, Eugene C., ed. "The Austin Papers." *Annual Report of the American Historical Association for the Year 1922 in Two Volumes.* Washington, D.C.: Government Printing Office, 1928.

———, ed. *The Austin Papers, 1834–1837,* vol. 3. Austin: University of Texas Press, 1926.

———. "The Career and Character of Stephen F. Austin." In Barker Papers, Box 2B109. Barker Texas History Center, Austin.

———. "Description of Texas by Stephen F. Austin." *Southwestern Historical Quarterly* 28 (1924): 98–121.

———. *The Life of Stephen F. Austin.* Austin: University of Texas Press, 1969.

———. "Stephen F. Austin." In *Readings in Texas History,* in Barker Papers, Box 2B107, "Articles, 1914–1918." Barker Texas History Center, Austin.

Barney, William. "The Cranes at Muleshoe." In *The Killdeer Crying: Selected Poems of William Barney.* Edited by Dave Oliphant. Fort Worth: Prickly Pear Press, 1977.

Barr, Ameila E. *All the Days of My Life.* New York: Appleton, 1913.

Bartlett, John Russell. *Personal Narrative of Explorations and Incidents in Texas, New Mexico, California, Sonora and Chihuahua.* 2 vols. Chicago: Rio Grande Press, 1965.

Bedichek, Roy. *Adventures with a Texas Naturalist.* New York: American Museum of Natural History, 1961.

Benson, Nettie Lee. "Bishop Marín de Porras and Texas." *Southwestern Historical Quarterly* 51 (1947): 16–40.

Berger, Max. *The British Traveller in America, 1836–1860.* New York: Columbia University Press, 1943.

Biesele, Rudolph L. *The History of the German Settlements in Texas, 1831–1861.* Austin: von Boeckmann-Jones, 1930.

Blegen, Theodore C. *Land of Their Choice: The Immigrants Write Home.* Minneapolis: University of Minnesota Press, 1955.

———. *Norwegian Migration to America: 1825–1860.* 2 vols. Northfield, Minn.: Norwegian-American Historical Association, 1931.

Bollaert, William. "Observations on the Geography of Texas." *Journal of the Royal Geographical Society* 20 (1850): 113–35.

Bonnell, George W. *Topographical Description of Texas.* Waco, Tex.: Texian Press, 1964.

Brereton, Lewis H. "American Indians of the Southeast and Southwest in the Works of Charles Sealsfield, Karl May and Friedrich Armand Strubberg." Master's thesis, University of Texas at Austin, 1969.

Brown, D. J. "Encouragement of Agriculture in the United States." In U.S. Patent Office, *Report of the Commissioner of Patents for the Year 1857,* pp. 15–29. Washington, D.C.: Harris, 1858.

Buckley, Samuel B. "Grapes and Grape Culture in Texas." *Texas Almanac for 1868*, pp. 23, 69.

——. *A Preliminary Report of the Geological and Agricultural Survey of Texas.* Austin: "State Gazette," 1866.

——. *Second Annual Report of the Geological and Agricultural Survey of Texas.* Houston: Gray, 1876.

Bugbee, Lester G. "The Old Three Hundred." *Quarterly of the Texas State Historical Association* 1 (1897): 108–17.

Bunkše, Edmunds V. "Commoner Attitudes toward Landscape and Nature." *Annals of the Association of American Geographers* 68 (1978): 551–66.

Burkhalter, Lois Wood. *Gideon Lincecum, 1793–1874: A Biography.* Austin: University of Texas Press, 1965.

Burnam, Jesse. "Reminiscences of Capt. Jesse Burnam." *Quarterly of the Texas State Historical Association* 5 (1901): 12–18.

Buttimer, Anne. "Grasping the Dynamism of the Lifeworld." *Annals of the Association of American Geographers* 66 (1976): 277–92.

Carlson, Paul H. *Texas Woollybacks: The Range Sheep and Goat Industry.* College Station: Texas A&M University Press, 1982.

Chinard, Gilbert. "Eighteenth Century Theories on America as a Human Habitat." *Proceedings of the American Philosophical Society* 91 (1947): 27–57.

Clausen, C. A., ed. *The Lady with the Pen.* Northfield, Minn.: Norwegian-American Historical Association, 1961.

Conway, Alan, ed. *The Welsh in America.* Minneapolis: University of Minnesota Press, 1961.

Coppini, Pompeo. *From Dawn to Sunset.* San Antonio: Naylor, 1949.

Cosgrove, Denis. *Social Formation and Symbolic Landscape.* London: Croom Helm, 1984.

Cutrer, Thomas W. *The English Texans.* San Antonio: Institute of Texan Cultures, 1985.

Dale, Edward Everett. *The Cross Timbers: Memories of a North Texas Boyhood.* Austin: University of Texas Press, 1966.

De Leon, Arnoldo. *They Called Them Greasers: Anglo Attitudes toward Mexicans in Texas, 1821–1900.* Austin: University of Texas Press, 1983.

Dewees, William B. *Letters from an Early Settler of Texas.* Waco, Tex.: Texian Press, 1968.

Dodge, Richard Irving. *The Hunting Grounds of the Great West.* London: Chatto and Windus, 1878.

Domenech, Emanuel H. Dieudonne. *Missionary Adventures in Texas.* London: Longman, Brown, Green, 1858.

Doughty, Robin W. *Wildlife and Man in Texas: Environmental Change and Conservation.* College Station: Texas A&M University Press, 1983.

Durand, Herbert. *The City of Missions, San Antonio, Texas.* St. Louis: Woodward and Tiernan, 1894.

BIBLIOGRAPHY

Edward, David B. *The History of Texas.* Cincinnati: J. A. James, 1836.
Edwards, Mary Jo. "Texas Agriculture as Reflected in Letters to the Southern Cultivator Prior to 1861." Master's thesis, East Texas Teachers College, 1948.
Fehrenbach, T. R. *Lone Star: A History of Texas and the Texans.* New York: Collier, 1980.
Fenley, Florence. *Oldtimers of Southwest Texas.* Uvalde, Tex.: Hornby, 1957.
Ferris, George A. "Stock Raising in Texas." *Texas Rural Almanac.* Houston: Hardcastle, 1876.
Fischer, Ernest G. *Marxists and Utopias in Texas.* Burnet, Tex.: Eakin Press, 1980.
Fisher, Orceneth. *Sketches of Texas in 1840.* Springfield: Ill.: Walters and Weber, 1841.
Flannery, John B. *The Irish Texans.* San Antonio: Institute of Texan Cultures, 1980.
Gaillardet, Théodore-Frédéric. *Sketches of Early Texas and Louisiana.* Austin: University of Texas Press, 1966.
Galveston Bay and Texas Land Company. *An Address to Emigrants.* Boston: N.p., 1835.
Galveston, Harrisburg, and San Antonio Railway Co. *Immigrants Guide to Western Texas: Sunset Route.* Boston: Lawrence, 1876.
————. *Western Texas as a Winter Resort.* Chicago: Rand, McNally, 1878.
Gates, Paul W. *The Farmer's Age: Agriculture, 1815–1860.* New York: Holt, Rinehart and Winston, 1960.
Geiser, Samuel W. *Horticulture and Horticulturists in Early Texas.* Dallas: Southern Methodist University Press, 1945.
————. *Naturalists of the Frontier.* 2nd ed., rev. Dallas: Southern Methodist University Press, 1948.
Glacken, Clarence J. "Count Buffon on Cultural Changes of the Physical Environment." *Annals of the Association of American Geographers* 50 (1960): 1–21.
————. *Traces on the Rhodian Shore.* Berkeley and Los Angeles: University of California Press, 1967.
Goetzmann, William H. *Exploration and Empire: The Explorer and the Scientist in the Winning of the American West.* New York: Knopf, 1966.
Goetzmann, William H., and Joseph C. Porter. *The West as Romantic Horizon.* Lincoln: University of Nebraska Press, 1981.
Goyen, William. *The House of Breath.* New York: Random House, 1950.
Greene, A. C. *A Personal Country.* New York: Knopf, 1969.
Gregg, Josiah, *The Commerce of the Prairies.* Edited by Milo Milton Quaife. Lincoln: University of Nebraska Press, 1967.
Guice, C. Norman. "Texas in 1804." *Southwestern Historical Quarterly* 59 (1955): 46–56.
"On Gulf States and the Amazon." *De Bow's Review* 18 (1855): 91–93.

Haley, J. Evetts. *The XIT Ranch of Texas and the Early Days of the Llano Estacado.* Norman: University of Oklahoma Press, 1953.

Hammond, William, and Margaret Hammond. *La Reunion: A French Settlement in Texas.* Dallas: Royal, 1958.

Hanson, John W. *The American Italy: Southern California.* Chicago: Conkey, 1896.

Harris, Benjamin Butler. *The Gila Trail: Texas Argonauts and the California Gold Rush.* Edited by Richard H. Dillon. Norman: University of Oklahoma Press, 1960.

Hartnel, Richard, comp. *Texas and California.* London: Smith, Elder, 1841.

Hatcher, Mattie A. *The Opening of Texas to Foreign Settlement, 1801–1821.* University of Texas Bulletin, no. 2714. Austin: University of Texas Press, 1927.

Hedrick, U. P. *A History of Horticulture in America to 1860.* New York: Oxford University Press, 1950.

Heidegger, Martin. *Poetry, Language, Thought.* Translated by Albert Hofstadter. New York: Harper and Row, 1971.

Holley, Mary Austin. *Mary Austin Holley: The Texas Diary, 1835–1838.* Edited by J. P. Bryan. Austin: University of Texas Press, 1965.

———. *Texas.* Austin: Steck, 1935.

———. *Texas: Observations Historical, Geographical and Descriptive in a Series of Letters.* Baltimore: Armstrong and Plaskitt, 1833.

Hollon, W. Eugene, and Ruth L. Butler, eds. *William Bollaert's Texas.* Norman: University of Oklahoma Press, 1956.

Hooton, Charles, *St. Louis' Isle, or Texiana.* London: Simmonds and Ward, 1847.

Houstoun, Matilda Charlotte F. *Texas and the Gulf of Mexico.* Austin: Steck-Warlick, 1968.

Huber, Armin O. "Frederic Armand Strubberg, Alias Dr. Shubbert, Town Builder, Physician and Adventurer, 1806–1889." *West Texas Historical Association Yearbook* 38 (1962): 37–71.

Hughes, J. Donald. *American Indian Ecology.* El Paso: Texas Western Press, 1983.

Humboldt, Alexander von. *Cosmos: A Sketch of a Physical Description of the Universe.* Translated by E. C. Otte. 5 vols. New York: Harper, 1860.

Hunter, J. Marvin. *The Trail Drivers of Texas.* 2nd ed., rev. Nashville: Cokesbury, 1925.

Huson, Hobart. *The Refugio Colony and Texas Independence.* Refugio, Tex.: N.p., 1936.

Ikin, Arthur. *Texas: Its History, Topography, Agriculture, Commerce, and General Statistics.* Waco, Tex.: Texian Press, 1964.

"Internal Improvements in Texas." *De Bow's Review* 6 (1848): 364–65.

Jackson, John B. *American Space: The Centennial Years, 1865–1876.* New York: Norton, 1972.

Johnson, James T. "Hardships of a Cowboy's Life in the Early Days of Texas." In *The Trail Drivers of Texas*. Edited by J. M. Hunter. 2nd ed. Nashville: Cokesbury, 1925.

Jones, Billy M. "A Burden on the Southwest: Migrant Tuberculars in the Nineteenth Century." *Southwestern Social Science Quarterly* 47 (1966): 59–67.

———. *Health-Seekers in the Southwest, 1817–1900*. Norman: University of Oklahoma Press, 1967.

Jordan, Terry G., and Marlis A. Jordan, eds. "Letters of a German Pioneer in Texas." *Southwestern Historical Quarterly* 60 (1966): 463–72.

Kelton, Elmer. *The Time It Never Rained*. Garden City, N.Y.: Doubleday, 1973.

Kendall, George W. *Across the Great Southwestern Prairies*. 2 vols. N.p.: Readex Microprint, 1974.

Kennedy, William. *Texas: The Rise, Progress, and Prospects of the Republic of Texas*. 2nd ed. Fort Worth: Molyneaux, 1925.

King, C. Richard, ed. *Victorian Lady on the Texas Frontier: The Journal of Ann Raney Coleman*. Norman: University of Oklahoma Press, 1971.

King, Edward. *The Great South*. Baton Rouge: Louisiana State University Press, 1972.

Kolodny, Annette. *The Land before Her: Fantasy and Experience of the American Frontier, 1630–1860*. Chapel Hill: University of North Carolina Press, 1984.

———. *The Lay of the Land*. Chapel Hill: University of North Carolina Press, 1975.

Kuykendall, J. H. "Reminiscences of Early Texans, II." *Quarterly of the Texas State Historical Association* 6 (1903): 311–30; and 7 (1903–1904): 29–64.

[Lawrence, A. B.]. *Texas in 1840, or, The Emigrant's Guide to the New Republic*. New York: Arno Press, 1973.

Lee, Daniel. "Progress of Agriculture in the United States." in U.S. Patent Office, *Report of the Commissioner of Patents for the Year 1852, Part II — Agriculture*, pp. 1–22. Washington, D.C.: Armstrong, 1853.

Lee, Rebecca Smith. *Mary Austin Holley: A Biography*. Austin: University of Texas Press, 1962.

"Letters Describing a Ride through Texas." *Sidney's Emigrant's Journal and Traveller's Magazine* (1850). Typed manuscript in L. B. Friend, Papers, Box 3F409, Professional Activities: Texas Subject File, *Emigrants Journal*. Barker Texas History Center, Austin.

"Letters from Texas." *Sidney's Emigrant's Journal and Traveller's Magazine* 5. Typed manuscript in L. B. Friend, Papers, Box 3F409, Professional Activities: Texas Subject File. *Emigrants Journal*. Barker Texas History Center, Austin.

Lummis, Charles F. *The Spanish Pioneers*. Chicago: McClurg, 1920.

Lundy, Benjamin. *The Life, Travels and Opinions of Benjamin Lundy, Including His Journeys to Texas and Mexico*. New York: Negro Universities Press, 1969.

Lyell, Charles. *Principles of Geology: Being an Inquiry How Far the Former Changes of the Earth's Surface Are Referable to Causes Now in Operation.* 2 vols. Philadelphia: Kay, 1837.

———. *Principles of Geology; or, the Modern Changes of the Earth and its Inhabitants Considered as Illustrative of Geology.* 11th ed., rev. 2 vols. New York: Appleton, 1887.

McClintock, William A. "Journal of a Trip through Texas and Northern Mexico in 1846–1847, II." *Southwestern Historical Quarterly* 34 (1930): 141–58.

McDaniel, H. F., and N. A. Taylor. *The Coming Empire; or, Two Thousand Miles in Texas on Horseback.* New York: Barnes, 1877.

McGregor, Stuart. "The Texas Almanac, 1857–1873." *Southwestern Historical Quarterly* 50 (1947): 419–30.

McMurtry, Larry. "Ever a Bridegroom: Reflections on the Failure of Texas Literature." *Texas Observer* (October 23, 1981): 1, 8–19.

Maillard, N. Doran. *The History of the Republic of Texas.* London: Smith, Elder, 1842.

Malone, Ann P. *Women on the Texas Frontier.* El Paso: Texas Western Press, 1983.

Marcy, Randolph B. *The Prairie Traveller.* New York: Harper, 1859.

Marsh, George Perkins. *Man and Nature: Or, Physical Geography as Modified by Human Action.* Edited by David Lowenthal. Cambridge: Harvard University Press, 1965.

Marx, Leo. "Pastoral Ideals and City Troubles." In *Western Man and Environmental Ethics.* Edited by Ian G. Barbour, pp. 93–115. Reading, Mass.: Addison-Wesley, 1973.

Mason, Charles. "Report of the Commissioner of Patents." in U.S. Patent Office, *Report of the Commissioner of Patents for the Year 1856.* Washington, D.C.: Wendell, 1857.

Maury, Matthew Fontaine. "Great Commercial Advantages of the Gulf of Mexico." *De Bow's Review* 7 (1849): 510–23.

———. *Physical Geography of the Sea.* New York: Harper, 1855.

Mesick, Jane L. *The English Traveller in America, 1785–1835.* New York: Columbia University Press, 1922.

Miller, Perry. *Errand into the Wilderness.* Cambridge, Mass.: Belknap, 1956.

"Miscellany." *De Bow's Review* 32 (1866): 211.

Missouri, Kansas, and Texas Railway Co. *Sunny San Antonio.* Chicago: Missouri, Kansas, and Texas Passenger Traffic Department, 1911.

Missouri Pacific Railway Co. *San Antonio as a Health and Pleasure Resort.* St. Louis: Woodward and Tiernan, ca. 1901.

Mott, Frank L. *A History of American Magazines.* 4 vols. Cambridge: Harvard University Press, 1957.

Muir, Andrew F., ed. *Texas in 1837.* Austin: University of Texas Press, 1958.

Munson, Thomas Volney. *Foundations of American Grape Culture.* Denison, Tex.: Munson, 1909.

Newcomb, Rexford. *Mediterranean Domestic Architecture in the United States.* Cleveland: Jansen, 1928.

———. *The Spanish House for America.* Philadelphia: Lippincott, 1927.

Norberg-Schulz, Christian. *Genius Loci: Toward a Phenomenology of Architecture.* New York: Rizzoli, 1980.

Nunn, W. C. "A Journal of Our Trip to Texas, October 6, 1853, by Mary James Eubank." *Texana* 10 (1972): 30–44.

Nuttall, Thomas. *A Manual of the Ornithology of the United States and Canada.* 2nd ed. Boston: Hilliard, Gray, 1840.

Nuttall, Zelia, "Royal Ordinances Concerning the Laying Out of New Towns." *Hispanic American Historical Review* 4 (1921): 743–45.

Oliphant, Dave, ed. *The Killdeer Crying: Selected Poems of William Barney.* Fort Worth: Prickly Pear Press, 1977.

Olmsted, Frederick Law. *A Journey through Texas.* Austin: University of Texas Press, 1978.

Owens, William A. *A Season of Weathering.* New York: Scribner's, 1973.

———. *This Stubborn Soil: A Frontier Boyhood.* London: Faber and Faber, 1966.

Parker, Amos A. *Trip to the West and Texas.* New York: Arno, 1973.

Parker, William B. *Notes Taken during the Expedition Commanded by Captain R. B. Marcy.* Philadelphia: Hayes and Zell, 1856.

Patton, Clyde P., Charles S. Alexander, and Fritz L. Kramer. *Physical Geography.* Belmont, Calif.: Wadsworth, 1970.

Peyton, Green. *San Antonio: City in the Sun.* New York: McGraw-Hill, 1946.

Pratt, Willis W., ed. *Galveston Island; or, a Few Months off the Coast of Texas: The Journal of Francis C. Sheridan, 1839–1840.* Austin: University of Texas Press, 1954.

"Public Lands of Texas." *De Bow's Review* 13 (1852): 53–56.

Qualey, Carlton C. *Norwegian Settlement in the United States.* Northfield, Minn.: Norwegian-American Historical Association, 1938.

Rabb, Mary Crownover. *Travels and Adventures in Texas in the 1820S.* Waco, Tex.: Morrison, 1962.

Raunick, Selma M. "A Survey of German Literature in Texas." *Southwestern Historical Quarterly* 33 (1929): 134–59.

Reclus, Elisee. *The Earth and Its Inhabitants: Europe.* 19 vols. New York: Appleton, 1883–1895.

Rejebian, Ermance V. "La Réunion: The French Colony in Dallas County." *Southwestern Historical Quarterly* 43 (1940): 472–78.

Relph, Edward. *Place and Placelessness.* London: Pion, 1976.

———. *Rational Landscapes and Humanistic Geography.* London: Croom Helm, 1981.

"Resources and Progress of Texas." *De Bow's Review* 4 (1847): 318–25.

Roberts, O. M. *A Description of Texas.* St. Louis: Gilbert, 1881.

Robinson, Willard B. *Gone from Texas: Our Lost Architectural Heritage.* College Station: Texas A&M University Press, 1981.

Roemer, Ferdinand von. *Texas: With Particular Reference to German Immigration and the Physical Appearance of the Country.* Translated by Oswald Mueller. San Antonio: Standard, 1935.

Roland, Charles P., and Richard C. Robbins, eds. "The Diary of Eliza (Mrs. Albert Sidney) Johnston." *Southwestern Historical Quarterly* 60 (1957): 463–500.

St. John, Percy Bolingbroke. "Bentley's Miscellany." *Campbell's Foreign Semi-Monthly Magazine* 4 (1843): 510–16. Typed manuscript in L. B. Friend, Papers, Box 3F409, Professional Activities: Texas Subject File, *Emigrants Journal.* Barker Texas History Center, Austin.

Sánchez, José María. "A Trip to Texas in 1828." Translated by C. E. Castañeda. *Southwestern Historical Quarterly* 29 (1926): 249–88.

Scarborough, Dorothy. *The Wind.* New York: Harper, 1925.

Schutze, A. E. *The Summer Birds of Central Texas.* Austin: Schutz, 1901.

Seamon, David. *A Geography of the Lifeworld: Movement, Rest and Encounter.* New York: St. Martin's Press, 1979.

Seele, Hermann. *The Cypress and Other Writings of a German Pioneer in Texas.* Austin: University of Texas Press, 1979.

Selle, Ralph A. *El Jardin: Birds Sing in Texas.* Houston: Carroll, 1934.

Semple, Ellen C. *The Geography of the Mediterranean Region.* New York: AMS Press, 1931.

Sewell, Ernestine P. "La Reunion." In *The Folklore of Texan Cultures.* Edited by Francis E. Abernethy. Austin: Encino Press, 1974.

Shaw, Albert. *Icaria: A Chapter in the History of Communism.* Philadelphia: Porcupine Press, 1972.

Shipman, Daniel. *Frontier Life: 58 Years in Texas.* Pasadena, Tex.: Abbotsford, 1965.

Sibley, Marilyn M. "The Queen's Lady in Texas." *East Texas Historical Journal* 6 (1968): 109–23.

Smith, Ashbel. "Agriculture in Texas." *De Bow's Review* 18 (1855): 200–201.

Smith, Edward. "Account of a Journey through Northeastern Texas." *East Texas Historical Journal* 7 (1969): 28–49, 78–109; and 8 (1970): 29–91.

Smithwick, Noah. *The Evolution of a State.* Austin: University of Texas Press, 1983.

Spence, Mary Lee. "British Impressions of Texas and Texans." *Southwestern Historical Quarterly* 70 (1966): 163–83.

Stanley, I. H. S. "Sorghum Canes." In U.S. Patent Office, *Report of the Commissioner of Patents for the Year 1857,* p. 223. Washington, D.C.: Harris, 1858.

Stevenson, Charles H. "Report on the Coast Fisheries of Texas." In U.S. Commissioner of Fish and Fisheries, *Report of the Commissioner for 1889 to 1891,* p. 403. Washington, D.C.: Government Printing Office, 1893.

Stiff, Edward. *The Texan Emigrant: Being a Narration of the Adventures of the Author in Texas.* Waco, Tex.: Texian Press, 1968.

Sweet, Alexander E., and J. Amory Knox. *On a Mexican Mustang, through Texas, from the Gulf to the Rio Grande.* Hartford, Conn.: Scranton, 1883.

Sweet, George H. *Texas: Her Early History, Climate, Soil and Material Resources.* New York: O'Keefe, 1871.

Taylor, M. K. "The Climate of Southwestern Texas and Its Advantages as a Winter Health Resort." *Transactions of the American (Clinical and) Climatological Association* 5 (1888): 209–22.

"The Texas." *Quarterly Review* 61 (1838): 326–62.

"Texas." *De Bow's Review* 10 (1851): 627–45.

"Texas." *De Bow's Review* 14 (1853): 68.

Texas Almanac for 1858. Galveston: Richardson, 1857.

Texas Almanac for 1868. Galveston: Richardson, 1867.

Texas Emigration and Land Company. *Emigration to Texas.* London: Richardson, 1843.

"Texas—Her Natural Advantages—Wool and Factories." *De Bow's Review* 10 (1851): 464.

"Texas Items." *Southern Cultivator* 16 (1858): 369.

"Texas—Its Resources, Lands, Rivers, Products, Etc." *De Bow's Review* 9 (1850): 195–97.

"Texas Lands." *De Bow's Review* 8 (1850): 63–65.

"A Tour through Texas." *New Monthly Magazine* 131 (1864): 245.

Tuan, Yi-Fu. *Topophilia: A Study of Environmental Perception, Attitudes, and Values.* Englewood Cliffs, N.J.: Prentice-Hall, 1974.

United States, Patent Office. *Report of the Commissioner of Patents for the Year 1848.* Washington, D.C.: Wendell and Van Benthuysen, 1849.

———. *Report of the Commissioner of Patents for the Year 1857.* Washington, D.C.: Harris, 1858.

United States, War Department. *Adventure on Red River.* Edited and annotated by Grant Foreman. Norman: University of Oklahoma Press, 1937.

Unstad, Lyder L. "Norwegian Migration to Texas: A Historic Resume with Four 'American Letters.'" *Southwestern Historical Quarterly* 43 (1939): 176–95.

"The Valley of the Rio Grande." *De Bow's Review* 2 (1846): 363.

Vielé, Teresa. *Following the Drum: A Glimpse of Frontier Life.* Austin: Steck-Vaughn, 1968.

Vines, Robert A. *Trees, Shrubs, and Woody Vines of the Southwest.* Austin: University of Texas Press, 1960.

A Visit to Texas. Austin: Steck, 1952.

von Hineuber, Caroline. "Life of German Pioneers in Early Texas." *Quarterly of the Texas State Historical Association* 2 (1899): 227–32.

Wallis, Jonnie L. *Sixty Years on the Brazos: The Life and Letters of Dr. John Washington Lockhart.* Los Angeles: Wallis, 1930.

Waugh, Julia Nott. *Castro-Ville and Henri Castro, Empresario.* San Antonio: Standard, 1934.

Weber, Paul C. *America in Imaginative German Literature in the First Half of the Nineteenth Century.* New York: Columbia University Press, 1926.

Williams, Amelia W., and Eugene C. Barker, eds. *The Writings of Sam Houston, 1813–1863,* vol. 5. Austin: University of Texas Press, 1941.

Williams, H. C. "Native Grapes of Arkansas and Texas." in U.S. Patent Office, *Report of the Commissioner of Patents for the Year 1859: Agriculture,* pp. 30–41. Washington, D.C.: Bowman, 1860.

Wood, W. D. "Reminiscences of Texas and Texans Fifty Years Ago." *Southwestern Historical Quarterly* 5 (1901): 113–20.

———. "Sketches of the Early Settlement of Leon County." *Southwestern Historical Quarterly* 4 (1901): 203–17.

Woodman, David. *Guide to Texas Emigrants.* Waco, Tex.: Texian Press, 1974.

Wraxall, C. F. Lascelles, ed. *The Backwoodsman; or, Life on the Indian Frontier.* Boston: Burnham, 1866.

Wright, John K. "Terrae Incognitae: The Place of Imagination in Geography." *Annals of the Association of American Geographers* 37 (1947): 1–15.

Wright, Louis B. *Culture on the Moving Frontier.* New York: Harper, 1961.

Zuber, William. *My Eighty Years in Texas.* Austin: University of Texas Press, 1971.

Index

At Home in Texas was composed into type on a Compugraphic photo-typesetter in ten point Garamond with two points of spacing between the lines. Garamond was also selected for display. The book was designed by Jim Billingsley, composed by Metricomp, Inc., printed offset by Thomson-Shore, Inc., and bound by John H. Dekker & Sons. . The paper on which this book is printed bears acid-free characteristics, for an effective life of at least three hundred years.

TEXAS A&M UNIVERSITY PRESS : COLLEGE STATION